'An exceptional book that ~~~~~ ~~~~~ ~~~ importance of confidence in yourself, and your purpose for those key encounters in business. The importance of preparation, in demonstrating the confidence as a Top Dog. And the elimination of fear from your vocabulary. It is a real differentiator of executives in their encounters in the marketplace.'

Jim Knauss, Global Vice Chair, Global Markets Business Development, Ernst & Young Global Limited

'You can't possibly succeed in business or your personal life unless you know how to persuade. This book tells you how it's done. A revelation.'

Drayton Bird, Chairman of Drayton Bird Associates. ex-Worldwide Creative Director and Vice Chairman, Ogilvy & Mather Direct

'If everybody who'd presented to me over the years had read this book first, I'd have been much more likely to do what they wanted!'

Julie Scott, Head of Operations, Standard Life

'Becoming a more successful and skilled communicator has never been more fun and relevant in today's business world. This book has a brilliant way of helping you think differently — and improve your performance — through engaging stories and insights that everyone can relate to. And, more importantly, actually *do*.

One of the authors (Andy) has helped my organization deliver a blockbusting performance over the last two years — through his language and techniques. In fact, we now use 'AndyBounds' as an adjective in our organization to denote the very best way to communicate and get the outcome you desire —"that presentation isn't 'AndyBounds' enough" and so on.

Top Dog is an excellent book. It will help you become a more successful business person.'

Colin Tyrer, National Sales Manager,
Top 10 Pharmaceutical Company

'The ultimate resource for selling yourself and your business effectively; and turning referrals into sales! This book — in a consistently insightful, practical, yet delightfully humorous manner — shows you how to ensure that your sales presentations always hit the mark for dramatically increased sales. My advice to you? Read this book before your competition does.'

Ivan Misner, Ph.D., NY Times Bestselling
Author and Founder of BNI®

'Top Dog is packed with practical, "real" advice — written with clarity, consistency and simplicity — to help improve your ability to persuade. There is business value on each and every page. An outstanding book.'

Andy Fell, General Manager,
St George Retail Bank

'An impactful, inspirational book: *Top Dog* is packed with a plethora of practical, effective solutions to your communication issues… including to some you never knew you had!'

> Julie Taylor, Strategy & Implementation Director, Sales & Marketing, Virgin Money

'This book will transform how you think about communicating with people, especially in potentially stressful situations. More importantly, it will transform how you do it.'

> Julian Mash, Founder and Chief Executive, Vision Capital

'Everyone wants to be the Top Dog; or to be able to influence the Top Dog. After reading this book, you'll realize it's easier to do this than you think. *Top Dog* provides simple, easy to understand steps that will make you wonder why you weren't doing them all along. This stuff just works!'

> Alan Kenny, EMEA/APAC General Manager, Mimecast

'If you are reluctant or baffled by how to make new contacts, build relationships and win more work, then read *Top Dog*. It's supremely practical, thoroughly unpretentious, and mercifully quick to read. A gem for busy professionals.'

> Maeve Jackson, Marketing & BD Director, Farrer & Co

'This book will help you sell more. It contains a simple, step-by-step approach to impressing clients. Every page, I found myself thinking "this is exactly how people should sell. But nobody does." And we have worked with Andy — his ideas work!'

Geoff Barnes, Chief Executive Officer and President, Baker Tilly International

'This book is full of such simple advice that works. The ideas are presented in a way that literally anyone can take them on board and use — to develop either themselves or their business. I don't know anyone in the world who wouldn't benefit from reading his book.'

Charlie Lawson, UK National Director of BNI, the world's largest networking/referrals organization

'First impressions count. This book will ensure you make a great one not merely a good one.'

Michael Brown, Senior Partner, BLM Law

TOP DOG

Impress and influence everyone you meet

Andy Bounds and Richard Ruttle

CAPSTONE
A Wiley Brand

This edition first published 2015

© 2015 Andy Bounds Ltd and Richard Ruttle

Registered office
John Wiley and Sons Ltd, The Atrium, Southern Gate, Chichester, West Sussex, PO19 8SQ, United Kingdom

For details of our global editorial offices, for customer services and for information about how to apply for permission to reuse the copyright material in this book please see our website at www.wiley.com.

The right of the authors to be identified as the authors of this work has been asserted in accordance with the Copyright, Designs and Patents Act 1988.

Wiley publishes in a variety of print and electronic formats and by print-on-demand. Some material included with standard print versions of this book may not be included in e-books or in print-on-demand. If this book refers to media such as a CD or DVD that is not included in the version you purchased, you may download this material at http://booksupport.wiley.com. For more information about Wiley products, visit www.wiley.com.

Designations used by companies to distinguish their products are often claimed as trademarks. All brand names and product names used in this book and on its cover are trade names, service marks, trademark or registered trademarks of their respective owners. The publisher and the book are not associated with any product or vendor mentioned in this book. None of the companies referenced within the book have endorsed the book.

Limit of Liability/Disclaimer of Warranty: While the publisher and author have used their best efforts in preparing this book, they make no representations or warranties with the respect to the accuracy or completeness of the contents of this book and specifically disclaim any implied warranties of merchantability or fitness for a particular purpose. It is sold on the understanding that the publisher is not engaged in rendering professional services and neither the publisher nor the author shall be liable for damages arising herefrom. If professional advice or other expert assistance is required, the services of a competent professional should be sought.

Library of Congress Cataloging-in-Publication Data

Bounds, Andy.

Top dog : impress and influence everyone you meet / Andy Bounds and Richard Ruttle.

pages cm

ISBN 978-0-85708-609-9 (pbk.)

1. Business communication. 2. Communication in management. 3. Influence (Psychology) I. Ruttle, Richard. II. Title.

HF5718.B65883 2015

658.4'5–dc23

2014046329

A catalogue record for this book is available from the British Library.

ISBN 978-0-857-08609-9 (pbk)
ISBN 978-0-857-08608-2 (ebk) ISBN 978-0-857-08607-5 (ebk)

Cover design: Wiley

Cover image: ©patrimonio designs ltd/Shutterstock

Brush type: ©iralu/Shutterstock

Set in 12/14 pt Myriad Pro by Aptara

Printed in Great Britain by TJ International Ltd, Padstow, Cornwall, UK

Contents

From Andy
To my Top Dogs … Em, Meg, Jack, Maia and Tom x

From Richard
To my pack … Emma, Mat and Oli
Brook, Misty and Elsa

About the Authors

 **Andy Bounds** is an award-winning consultant, who's helped his customers win £billions. Author of best-sellers *The Snowball Effect* and *The Jelly Effect*, he has spent decades studying what makes communication work.

His skills and passion stem from the fact his mother is blind. This has given him a lifetime's experience of seeing communication from *the other person's* point of view – so critical if you want to become Top Dog.

To join Andy's online video club, and access hundreds of his videos explaining how to communicate/sell better, visit www.andyboundsonline.com.

 **Richard Ruttle** is a leading practitioner in developing Board-level relationships in some of the world's largest and most famous companies. He has created and delivered Relationship Development training programmes for Senior Executives in two of the world's largest professional services companies.

His consultancy expertise has helped his customers to deliver major transformation programmes, delivering huge cost savings and increased revenues.

Acknowledgements

Andy

I've enjoyed writing *Top Dog*. Thanks to everyone who's helped me.

To Richard: thank you – it has been a great experience to write with you, to share our ideas, and to see how you go about things.

Top Dog is my third book. As always, it wouldn't have been possible without the fabulous team at Capstone; and my two Emmas …

To my wonderful PA Emma Platt (soon-to-be Emma Thomas – congratulations Em and Julian) – you've had the 'joy' of making sure I have the time and headspace to write, as well as spending countless hours typing. Thank you!

To the amazing Mrs Bounds – Em, thanks for all your help, wisdom, insight and all-round brilliance. And for being so tactful when advising on edits!

And finally, to my four Top Pups: you make me proud every day …

Meg, you'll have a fab time at Uni – such an exciting time for you. Thanks for your advice on the book – it was invaluable.

Jack, thanks for going easy on me when we play sport. I know you let me win sometimes. But thanks for pretending you don't.

Super Maia, I just think you're fab. I can't wait for our next Daddy Daughter Date. Tell you what: you choose where we go, and I'll pay. OK?

And Tom, by the time you're old enough to read this, I'll hopefully have forgotten that you keep me awake so much. I'll do my best to have forgiven you by then too …

Richard

To Andy Bounds for his legendary and unending patience with me as a new writer, Bill from whom I learnt most and for cajoling and encouraging, Pamela and Steve for cheering me on when energy was flagging. So many others who have encouraged and supported.

To all my faithful canine companions – Jinny, Crispy, Biddy, Toby, Kentee, Temp, Corry , Elsa, Misty and Brook.

Most of all, my Grown Up kids – Emma whose focus on helping others less fortunate humbles me, Matt the new entrepreneur whose dedication and commitment inspires me and Oli whose dedication to fitness has pushed even me into the gym!

And of course … my Mum!

Introduction

When you have an important meeting coming up, how do you prepare?

Pull some materials together?

Create a new slide deck?

Prepare your opening line? Maybe 'thanks for sparing your time'?

People do things like this all the time. You see it every day.

But just because it's everywhere doesn't mean it's best.

For example, when you turn up with pre-prepared material or slides that they haven't asked for, they'll probably assume you intend to talk *at* them, not *with* them.

And phrases like 'thanks for sparing your time' can come across as deferential ('your time's more important than mine'); not equal.

The other person picks up on this. And, without doing a thing, they're now in charge. This means your conversation usually ends with what they want, not what you want. This could mean you don't get the pay rise you deserve; the sale; the new job; the promotion …

When this happens, in effect, you 'lost' before you even started talking.

People want you to be impressive, not subservient

If this sounds depressingly familiar, don't worry: you aren't alone. When pushed, most people would admit their approach doesn't differentiate them from anyone else. They also know that, unless they can establish peer-level relationships and credibility, they'll always lose to the Top Dog.

But other Top Dogs don't want you to be like this!

They want you to impress them. To help them. To add value to them. That's why they're seeing you.

And, since most of your competitors – both business and personal – struggle with this, it's a huge opportunity for you.

This book will help you take that opportunity.

You'll learn hundreds of new, simple, practical ways to impress and influence others – great for pay rises, sales, new jobs and promotions – including:

- Easy ways to impress from Minute One.
- How to prepare to have outstanding meetings and

interactions which appear spontaneous, but are in fact well-rehearsed.
- Practical advice around establishing rapport, using impactful Elevator Pitches and icebreakers that work but aren't cheesy.
- How to build your confidence, to convince yourself you're Top Dog – because, if you can't do that, you've little chance of convincing anyone else.
- Word-for-word scripts that help you overcome the challenges you hear every day.
- How to talk less about what you *do* ('I'm a tax expert') and more about the impact you *cause* ('I'll slash your tax bill'). Top Dogs love things like this.
- How to reinforce your messages by telling compelling stories focused on their agenda. They can relate to these much more than they can to traditional credentials presentations.
- Simple steps to preparing communications that impress, and achieve what you both want.

Why we chose to co-author the book

Both of us have helped thousands of people – and their businesses – become more successful through improved communication. But we've done so coming at it from very different angles …

Andy is an award-winning consultant, who's helped his customers win £billions. Author of best-sellers *The Snowball Effect* and *The Jelly Effect*, he has spent decades studying what makes communication work. His skills and passion stem from the fact his mother is blind. This has given him a lifetime's experience of seeing communication from *the other person's* point of view – so critical if you want to become Top Dog.

Richard is a leading practitioner in developing Board-level relationships in some of the world's largest and most famous companies. He has created and delivered Relationship Development training programmes for Senior Executives in two of the world's largest professional services companies. His consultancy expertise has helped his customers to deliver major transformation programmes, delivering huge cost savings and increased revenues.

We spent ages discussing the scope of the book. Should we write everything we know about every situation you might face? About getting pay rises, sales, new jobs and promotions; building relationships; networking; presenting; securing buy-in; building engagement; and so on? But, if we did that, the book would have been ridiculously long.

So, to keep it a sensible length, we chose to focus on the one situation that contains all the elements of persuasion: how to find, get in front of, impress and then convince a busy Top Dog Executive to buy from you.

You can only master this when you possess *all* the attributes of being a Top Dog. Choosing this as our example means you can apply the techniques to any situation where you want to persuade someone to do something – with a few tweaks, of course.

And finally …

By the way, if you're interested, we both originated about half the content, and then edited each other's bits. So we've (kind of) both written everything. Some of the examples are Andy's; the rest are Richard's. We chose not to bore you by saying which is which.

The dogs, however, are Richard's. He's owned and bred dogs all his life. Andy knows virtually nothing about dogs. His mum has – until recently – always had a guide dog. But they arrive ready trained; and they're his mum's anyway. He once saw a dog in a park. But that's about it.

1

Lead the pack

Focus on others' successes, not your own

The secret to impressing a Top Dog?

Do things that impress them.

But people don't, do they? In fact, they often do the opposite. This week alone, you'll have been underwhelmed by how someone communicated with you. Maybe you received a dreadful email, or a tactless comment. Maybe they wasted your time at a pointless meeting, or made you sit through a tedious presentation. These things happen all the time.

Even worse, people don't know they're doing it. Over the years, I've asked thousands of people two questions:

1. Do you think your communications are generally good?

2. Do you think everyone else's are generally good?

People always answer 'yes; no'. In other words 'I'm ok. It's everyone else who isn't'. This throws up a few points.

Firstly, it's mathematically impossible. How can most people be good at something; and – at the same time – most people be bad at it?

Secondly, it's clear that people don't communicate in ways that impress others.

Thirdly – devastatingly – what we hate, we do.

This last one sounds weird. But, when you think about, it's the only possible explanation. Since everyone thinks it's everyone else who's wrong, we all must do things to others that we hate them doing to us. For example, you'll hear people say:

> 'I hate watching a presenter use wordy slides. I just end up reading them as he speaks. However, when I'm presenting, I like to use wordy slides, to remind me what to say'.

> 'I don't know why I attended that meeting. The Chair made no effort to tell me why the agenda was relevant to me … And now it's time for me to chair my meeting. So let's crack-on with my agenda'.

> 'I have only two problems with my inbox: finding time to create my beautiful emails, and being forced to read everyone else's rubbish ones'.

There is a huge positive to this. Since most people don't communicate well, it's relatively straightforward for you to stand out from the crowd. A brilliant opportunity for you! Or, of course, for them – if you choose not to improve.

Want to be better with people? Learn from the masters – dogs

This sounds weird (bear with me): we can learn much about interacting with others from the way dogs relate to their peers.

Why dogs? Well, they're arguably the most successful species on the planet, next to us. They've established themselves in every corner of the world. They're in our homes – in front of our hearths; in many cases, on our beds. They demand and get walks, toys, treats, blankets and food.

There are millions of them already; and their population is on the rise. Not bad for creatures who look bemused when the squirrel they're chasing climbs a tree; or – like the legendary Fenton – when some deer don't fancy chatting with you (if you haven't seen it on YouTube, watch it – very funny).

Dogs have domesticated themselves by breeding with other more sociable wolves. Humans accelerated this process by breeding those with the highest level of social skills. So when I look at my dogs Misty, Brook and Elsa, I see 4,000 years of wolf ancestry, with the same instincts and chromosomes.

As a result, an extremely tolerant and cognitively advanced animal (except Elsa) has evolved.

These wolves dressed in dog suits have charmed their way into our lives and homes. They live in idle luxury as a result. And we can learn from this! (Don't worry – this isn't a book on the psychology of dogs. But I will sometimes refer to the way they interact with their peers or 'pack'. It's a useful analogy to explain how best to impress others more than you do now.)

Be the Top Dog, not just a pack member

> 'Life is like a dogsled team. If you ain't the lead, the scenery never changes'.
>
> *Lewis Grizzard*

Like wolves, dogs are pack animals. Interactions between a pack's individuals are complex. They occur with a strict hierarchy. The Alpha male is at the top with his mate, the Alpha female. These are the Top Dogs. Under them, pack positions constantly change as younger dogs challenge superiors at every opportunity. Movement occurs through displays of dominance and submission.

You see this mirrored in the behaviour of groups of humans. Alpha males and females are obvious when you see them. They tend to get more of what they want, and more often, than other pack animals.

As you adopt the techniques in this book, you'll become more of one yourself. And it's important you do. Many people 'lose' before they even *start* a conversation. They're too deferential early on. Their words and actions convey 'you're my superior', not 'you're my equal'. For example:

- Thanking someone for sparing their busy time transmits 'your time, Mrs Alpha Dog, is more important than mine'.
- Avoiding eye contact suggests 'you're too important to look at'.
- Being too quiet implies 'your words are more important than mine'.

These set you up as the Beta Dog. The other person picks up on it. And – *without doing anything* – they're in charge. They're the Alpha Dog (or 'Top Dog'). This results in the conversation going nearer to where they want, not where you want.

You'll have had this happen to you. For instance, remember your last meeting with someone you felt held all the power? Someone 'more important' than you? Maybe you wanted a pay rise or promotion? Or were hoping (praying) an important customer liked your pitch? Who got what they wanted from the conversation – you or them?

It's easy to become Top Dog

Since most people make this 'Beta Dog Mistake', you can differentiate yourself by not doing it. It's a question of unlearning the bad habits you've picked up over your professional life; and then learning techniques to establish yourself as Top Dog. *You* can become the Very Important Person in all your communications. Imagine the power of that!

By focusing, experimenting and improving how you communicate, you can dramatically enhance how you build relationships with others.

Even better, you can apply these techniques in every type of interaction – conversations, interviews, socializing, dating, sales, marketing, network building … in any context where you want to impress and influence others.

The first step, of course, is to break current bad habits. Chapter 2 explains how to start doing this.

Doggie Treats

Focus on others' successes, not your own

- The secret to success? Brilliant communication.
- The secret to brilliant communication? Do what the other person wants, not what everyone else does.
- Be useful, not subservient.
- When you think and act as their peer, it's more likely they'll treat you as one.
- Most people don't do this. So it's easy to stand out.

2

Drop!

Unlearn the bad habits that hold you back

You can't teach an old dog new tricks

When Misty was a puppy, all she wanted to do was sleep. She saw her owners as other puppies and playmates.

She didn't take much notice of what we asked her to do. Instead, her behaviour was focused on copying us. When we sat watching TV, she'd sit and watch TV. When we ate at the table, she wanted to eat at the table. When we went to a particular room, she followed us in.

When it was time for formal training, she quickly responded to basic commands like *sit* and *stay*. As she became more confident, she became more competent. She learned a few tricks of her own – her favourite is dribbling a football. She delights everyone with this.

Brook and Elsa arrived partly trained as mature dogs. Neither do tricks, other than on command. But both follow every routine you'd expect from a dog – sitting, staying, going left and right. But there's no improvisation.

As the old saying goes: you can't teach an old dog new tricks.

But as the new saying goes (OK, I made it up): new tricks win more love. In terms of entertainment and winning affection, Misty wins every time.

How we've learned 'me too' habits

Are you more like 'improvising Misty', or 'me-too Brook and Elsa'?

Most people would claim the former. But most are the latter. That's why it's called 'me too'.

During our working lives, we've all developed habits. We repeat them in our networking and relationship-building activities – usually unconsciously. We travel in packs for safety. We build slide decks to use as a crutch. We dress formally to meet informally dressed customers. We print agendas. We even send them in advance!

We do this because – like puppies – we learn from watching and copying others. Sometimes we've even been trained to do these things. There's nothing *wrong* with them. Often, they don't detract from effective meetings and encounters.

But they don't impress. Nor is there anything different about them; because everyone does them. They demonstrate a formulaic 'me too' approach that brands us as 'yet another business person'.

Self Test: How do you stack up?

These are all common practice, not best practice. How many do you do?

1. Prepare slide packs for meetings, even if nobody requested one.
2. Always take a 'leave behind' document, even if nobody requested one.
3. Prepare what you're going to say, not what you're going to ask.
4. When at networking events, travel in packs with colleagues so you don't have to speak to strangers.
5. In meetings, do most of the talking.
6. In conversations, think 'I must get my #1 priority across', rather than 'I must find her #1 priority'.
7. When asked 'what do you do?', provide a detailed list of all your products and services.

(continued)

8. When asked to prepare a communication, cut/paste from last time's rather than asking exactly what the reader wants you to include.
9. Do to others what you hate people doing to you – use wordy slides, chair tedious meetings, etc.
10. On slide 1, bullet point 1, use the immortal phrase 'we were founded in 1922'.

You *can* teach an old human new tricks

Our contacts' world is full of formulaic business people. You're probably just one of many they're meeting that day. It therefore brings enormous advantage when you stand out from the pack; are viewed as a peer; and are *liked*. After all, they'll probably assume your products and services are similar to your competitors'. It's whether you're liked and trusted that makes the real difference.

Being 'liked' doesn't come from being subservient. You want to be their peer; not their junior. Instead, being 'liked' results from:

- Talking as an equal.
- Demonstrating relevant insight.
- Being socially engaging.
- Focusing on the other person's desired outcomes.
- Mastering the lost skill of shutting up and listening.

The rest of the book explains how to master all these, and break your me-too habits.

To build intimacy and trust, go solo

A quick question: have you ever had a relationship with another human being? (I hope so. If not, you need a different book!)

Cast your mind back: how did that relationship start? On your first date, did you take a colleague along with you in case you were asked a question you couldn't answer?

No?

Why not?

Because that would just be completely *weird*?

Because you wanted to learn about the other person in a reasonably intimate atmosphere?

Also, bringing a friend on your date would mean numbers escalate. You bring a friend; so does she. Before you know it, there are four, six, eight of you having an un-intimate, meandering, go-nowhere chat.

It's the same in business. Tell the CEO there'll be two of you, and she'll likely ask her Head of Strategy or CFO to join. Even if she doesn't, as the lone person she'll feel outnumbered and less inclined to open up. Very few people discuss their challenges in front of their colleagues, no matter how good your interview technique. I certainly don't. And I bet you don't either.

So why *do* people take colleagues to first meetings?

The standard response is 'to cover all angles that might arise – so we can answer all questions'.

And this might be the case. In my experience though, a more honest answer would be: 'I feel nervous, so I'm taking my pal'.

But, even if 'because we can answer all questions' is your reason, it isn't a good one. You want your first meeting to trigger a second one. That's the only output that matters. So *not* answering all her questions is invaluable! It provides a hook for meeting again – maybe accompanied this time by expert colleagues.

And, because you're alone in Meeting One, you can't get into technical details. This forces you to probe more deeply and learn more about her needs – 'but what's the *cause* of this challenge you've mentioned?'

In short, you want this first meeting to trigger a second one. And that's most likely when you build genuine rapport, have a peer-level discussion, and demonstrate you really grasp her issues or challenges. You can provide solutions later.

Pre-prepared slide packs make things worse

If you prefer long words: slide packs are an obstacle to gaining intimacy and trust.

If you prefer short ones: you'll never have a good chat while she's watching you read stuff.

When meeting a new acquaintance, would you honestly take a slide pack to introduce yourself, your background and interests?

Or when meeting a friend in a coffee shop, would you bring out a slide pack explaining 'it's been a while since we caught up. So I wanted to explain what I've been doing and also show my understanding of what's going on in your life' (if you do this, I think I might know why your friends are always 'too busy' to see you!)

As well as being tedious and irrelevant, slide packs:

- Stifle conversation – she'll think 'I'd prefer to chat, not read'.
- Suggest you formed your views before the meeting – 'why are we meeting at all? Why not just email me your already formed views?'.
- Limit (stop?) broader discussion – 'I can't be bothered joining in'.
- Cause you to talk too much – 'please shut up'.

They are, almost without exception, a bad idea at a first meeting.

Of course, sometimes visuals can help explain certain things. In which case:

- Learn to draw your favourite slides in the meeting – this looks much more impressive.
- Individual slides kept in your briefcase and only brought out if appropriate can work well too.

- If you do have to use slides – and you don't – make sure you talk in conjunction with them; don't just *read* them.

It's essential to make change easy. Or you won't do it.

I could summarize this chapter very quickly:

People have bad habits. So change yours.

But bad habits are – by definition – embedded. They're hard to change. And desire alone isn't enough. We all know people who desire to lose weight, but struggle because of the 'Sunday night's pizza night' habit.

The secret to breaking habits is to

1. Identify the building-block steps to take.
2. Keep taking them.
3. If you falter, don't give in.

The next few chapters help you master (1) and (2). The final chapter addresses (3).

Let's start by looking at the first building block: impressive ways to secure meetings with a Top Dog.

Doggie Treats

Unlearn the bad habits that hold you back

- Most people have adopted 'me too' habits. They look and sound the same as everyone else.
- Many of these habits aren't best practice; they're just common practice.
- To stand out, you have to stop doing them. But breaking habits is hard. You'll have to be proactive, and work at it.
- Habit #1 to break: don't take colleagues to Meeting One. You're more likely to establish real intimacy if it's one-to-one.
- Habit #2 to break: lose the slides. They constrain discussion. Never more so than in a first meeting. They suggest you think you know the issues before you start. Which you don't. They're a really bad idea.

3

The welcome visitor

Make a good first impression

Meeting strangers isn't easy.

So, if you're like most people, you'll fall into one of two camps:

> You do what everyone else does – give your business card, shake hands, and politely ask '*how's business*?'; or

> You don't really know what to do. So, don't do anything – maybe reassuring yourself by saying things like '*I haven't time*' or '*It isn't important in my business*'.

Neither is good. One doesn't make much impression. The other doesn't make … well, anything.

Dogs find it easy to differentiate themselves. So, learn from them

When dogs see a stranger, they react according to their instincts and personalities:

> Misty willingly approaches them, ears cocked, tail wagging. She treats them like a well-known friend.

Brook's nervous. She'll keep her distance, ears back, not aggressive, just timid. Her tail might wag a little, but at half-mast.

Elsa flies towards you, ears flapping with a life of their own, tail rotating like a demented propeller. She runs in circles, jumps up and squeaks with excitement.

And who gets the best response? Misty. Every time. She's instantly welcomed and stroked – even by those who don't like dogs. She exudes friendliness and confidence. She never appears to be a threat.

Poor old Brook rarely gets a look-in, as it's unclear whether she's aggressive or timid. Elsa appears over-excitable – a mad little spaniel who can't stay still long enough to make new friends.

Friendly. Timid. Excitable. How would others describe you?

First impressions drive everything. So improve yours

First impressions set the tone for everything that follows.

Have a great start, and a successful outcome's likely. Have a bad one, and you're unlikely to recover.

Given how easy it is to be either same-old or do-nothing, here are the six steps of 'doing a Misty' and becoming everyone's favourite:

1. Use an icebreaker to establish rapport quickly.
2. Write a compelling Elevator Pitch (so not 'I'm an Accountant').
3. Use your appearance to impress.
4. Ensure your handshake turns people on, not off.
5. Give your business cards when you should, not when everyone does.
6. Be flexible, so you adapt to whatever's thrown at you.

Taking each in turn …

1. Use an icebreaker to establish rapport quickly

Have you ever attended an event – maybe a wedding reception – where you found yourself at the same table as one of your business targets?

If so, did you immediately hand over your business card? Or just shake hands and say hello? And was your icebreaker a pre-prepared slide deck, or a comment about a mutual connection – like the bride or groom?

Or when on one of those all-inclusive holidays with endless water sports facilities, and chatting to someone who turned out to be a potential customer, did you run back to your room for a glossy brochure?

No? Thought not. So why do people choose to start first meetings by laying slide packs and business cards on the table? It isn't what others want us to do. In business – as in life – it's important to connect on a social level before launching into a sales presentation. So leave the papers in the briefcase and the card in the wallet – at least until you've established rapport.

This sounds obvious, but can be hard to do well. For instance, how often do you use traditional, non-differentiating icebreakers?

- The weather.
- Traffic.
- Sport.
- Current affairs.

- Holidays.
- Your customers' results.
- The view from the window.

These are all decent standbys if you have nothing else. But none of these differentiate you from the pack. Instead, they convey you're 'one of those lot'.

When you think about it, the only point of your icebreaker is to establish rapport. And this only happens when you say something relevant to them. So you need to know something about them. This means, wherever possible, doing some research. Not loads. But definitely more than none.

There are so many sources of info, it's pretty easy to research people now. Social media, Facebook, Twitter and LinkedIn provide access to information on people's hobbies, age and where they live. You can use all this to tailor an icebreaker – though be careful not to sound like a stalker!

I once Googled a senior business leader who we were meeting for the first time. I found he was a keen hiker from his weekend cottage in the Derbyshire Peak District. The weekend before we met, I visited friends in Derbyshire, walking with them and eating in the best pub restaurant in the locality.

The day I met him was the first sunny day of spring. In commenting on this, I suggested he might be wishing he was walking in the Dales. This led to an animated conversation on the area, and our joint enjoyment of his favourite restaurant. We'd really connected before addressing our agenda.

You can also pick up information by looking at people's surroundings. Pictures of children or yachts or fast cars provide clues. However, don't do what one colleague did …

He was meeting a new CEO of a large company. He spotted a Native American wood carving like an eagle with two large white eyes in his office. His icebreaker was to comment on it and to enquire as to its origins. A good start! The CEO explained it was a gift from his staff when he recently left their Canadian Division. He told us the belief was that, if you paint over the white eyes with symbols of your dreams and aspirations, they will come true. The colleague's response: 'Well let's see if we can paint them together in this meeting'… yuk!

Two final things that help at the start of a meeting:

- Sit in the right place. Don't have the sun in your eyes. If with colleagues, spread out around the table to appear more collaborative than confrontational. Avoid 'salesman vs buyers'.
- When standing, be in the centre of the room and hold the space. This will make you appear more confident and give you greater presence. Beta Dogs hug the walls!

2. Write a compelling Elevator Pitch (so not 'I'm an Accountant')

Your Elevator Pitch sets the tone for how others perceive you and what you do. So they're important. Certainly important enough to spend time thinking about yours.

But people don't. That's why – when you ask someone 'what do you do?' – they say things like 'I'm a Consultant'.

The only answer I can think of to this is 'Oh. Are you?'

Well either that, or 'Between jobs, are you?'

Not the best.

When you first meet someone, she'll ask what you do. Your response is your Elevator Pitch – how you'd describe yourself quickly if in an elevator (though a better phrase than 'Elevator Pitch' is 'First Impression Pitch', because that's what it is).

But most peoples' are just so *dull*. They tend to say one of:

- A generic job title – I'm a Consultant, Accountant, Lawyer.
- Their company's name – I work for Consultancy X, Accountants Y, Lawyers Z.
- Their main deliverable – I consult with customers, prepare Tax Returns, work in litigation.

These don't differentiate – because everyone says them.

Nor do they impress. Because they are – well, unimpressive.

A much better approach is to focus on your AFTERs – why others are better-off *after* working with you.

For example, which of these would you rather speak to?

1. I'm a Consultant.
2. I consult with customers.
3. I help my customers sell more than they thought possible.

And these?

1. I'm an Accountant.
2. I prepare Tax Returns.
3. I help my customers pay less tax.

These?

1. I'm a Lawyer.
2. I work in litigation.
3. I keep my customers out of jail.

Also, it's better if others talk more than you do – especially early in the conversation (because you learn more about them; they like that you're interested; it's polite). So also use your Elevator Pitch to get her speaking:

Her: **What do you do?**

You: **I help my customers be more successful than they could be without me.**

Her: **What do you mean? (This is pretty much the only response she could give. She's certainly not going to say 'Oh. Do you?')**

You: **It depends on the customer. Why don't you tell me more about your business? I can then share my experiences that are most relevant to you.**

Her: **(Starts talking. Again, this is her only possible response. She certainly _won't_ say 'no, I'd rather you were irrelevant'.)**

Your Elevator Pitch and follow-up sentence are so important, they're worth writing now. Imagine someone asked 'what do you do?', how would you reply?

Elevator Pitch	
Follow-up sentence, to get her talking again	

3. Use your appearance to impress

Others will assume a lot about you based on your appearance – your success, attention to detail, similarity to them, personality etc. Their assumption might be wrong. But you don't know what it is because they won't tell you. If it's negative, you're in a bad place. And you haven't even said anything yet!

As you know, you should be standing tall, looking confident, smart and well groomed.

As you also know, we've all been the opposite – crouched down, fumbling with briefcases, arriving late, looking harassed. You aren't being the serene, majestic creature you know you can be.

These things are easy to get right of course – *if you prioritize them*.

For example, your clothing should fit well, look sharp and well cared for. Shoes must be polished, and not down at heel.

Arriving early for meetings avoids unnecessary stress. It helps you adapt to your surroundings. This shows in your face and demeanour. (As an aside: if you always arrive late for meetings, stop cramming in 'one more thing' before you leave the office.)

The majority of us dress up. Not only is this safer than being too casual, but many feel more comfortable in uniform. How we dress, however, can create a barrier. It's fairly common to see herds of suited-and-booted accountants, management consultants and software salespeople trooping through the corridors of creative companies looking decidedly out of place.

But others like you more if you're more like them. So, if you realize you're too formal, when finding your contact has no tie, remove yours and unbutton your shirt with a sigh of relief. This usually raises a welcome smile. This is Alpha Dog behaviour. It makes you appear flexible and relaxed.

4. Ensure your handshake turns people on, not off

For such a seemingly innocuous thing, a handshake has a big impact. For instance, is it just me, or have you ever thought: 'If you shake hands this limply, how can I expect you to get a firm grasp on my business?'

You'll have experienced many species of handshake on your travels – clammy, limp, or The Crusher, whose owner thinks it shows confidence and superiority, but actually makes you want to punch them.

So make sure yours is good. If your hands get clammy, don't just wipe them on your trousers – doesn't work. Instead carry one of those small tubes of hand sanitizer that keeps them dry. Or, if that feels ridiculous, wash your hands under the cold tap, then dry them in a warm air dryer.

You want your handshake to be firm enough to be comfortable, and at a controlled speed. Since you don't know what it's like to shake your own hand, ask a friend for feedback. Tell them to be honest, not nice.

5. Give your business cards when you should, not when everyone does

My dogs don't like to wear collars. But they have to wear them when they go out because of their identity disc with their name and my number. These discs are only useful if the dogs get lost and someone wants to contact me.

Business cards are like dog collars. They provide a name and contact details on a handy wallet-size card. People usually hand them out at the start of a meeting. Why?

- To say who you are? You can safely assume that, if your contact has troubled to meet you, they know your name and company.
- To show your job title and how important you are? This may not be as important to them as it is to you! And it can work against colleagues with junior titles.
- To provide follow-up details? Bingo! This means cards are more suited to being produced at the *end* of the meeting to cement next steps and actions. (Though if your contact produces a card at the outset, of course it's only polite to reciprocate.)

But just because you're clear what to do with a business card doesn't mean others are. Some think highly of their job title. Their card may encapsulate to them all that they've achieved professionally. So, when they hand it to you, treat it with respect. Take time to read it. Place it in a 'special' treasured place – in your purse or wallet, not just casually in a top pocket. Also, leaving it on the desk may suggest you can't remember who you're meeting with, or what they do.

6. Be flexible, so you adapt to whatever's thrown at you

Unfortunately, despite all your brilliant prep, sometimes things happen 'for a reason' (as mother would say).

For example, on a visit to a potential customer in the Midlands of England, I forgot to prepare my icebreaker. While on my mobile getting briefed by colleagues, I walked off the train straight into a taxi parked outside the station, breaking off my call only to give the driver the address.

The driver looked puzzled and said 'are you sure, sir?' Still on the phone, the answer was a slightly irritated 'yes, I am sure, thank you'.

At that point, the taxi did a perfect U-turn and stopped. He stepped out, opened the door and pointed to a huge company logo over the entrance to a building immediately opposite the station. 'That will be £1 please sir. Would you like a receipt?'

When the Finance Director met me in reception, he asked if I'd been there before. My response was 'no – I actually took a taxi here from the station'. It turned out to be a great icebreaker. He explained animatedly just how much he and his family disliked the town. We became firm friends – and remain so – before we discussed anything relating to commerce.

And now your first impression's so much better, let's use it

Do everything in this chapter, and you'll instantly come across as a differentiated Top Dog.

The key now is to get away from your desk, and start doing it. The next chapter shows simple ways to get meetings with other Top Dogs; and how to prepare for them so they go brilliantly on the day.

Doggie Treats

Make a good first impression

- Improve your first impression. The way you look, carry yourself, shake hands and introduce yourself differentiates you – especially since most people don't do it well.
- Personalized, interesting icebreakers establish rapport quickly. They set the tone for building a long-term relationship, not a short-term sales presentation.
- Base your Elevator Pitch on your AFTERs …
- … and use it to get the other person talking about themselves and their priorities.
- Establish rapport before getting into subject matter. Do this based on your personality and social skills, not your job title.

**4**

Pick up the lead

Get – then prepare for – a great first
meeting

Think of a recent meeting that had no clear agenda. Let me guess – one of three things happened:

- It became very one-sided, with the customer telling you how well they were doing and that everything was rosy.
- It became very one-sided, with you or your colleagues asking lots of questions and getting a poor response.
- It was a meandering, pointless mess that resulted in no actions.

I think the worst meeting I attended was many years ago. I was a junior team member meeting a Senior Executive of a global bank. We kept asking questions, culminating in the toe-curling 'what keeps you awake at night?' The Executive replied 'at the moment, a very pretty Californian blonde. Now gentlemen, I need to end this meeting'.

Ouch. We hadn't given him any value. We hadn't earned the right to interrogate him like that. We were working as a pack. We hadn't set the context for the meeting. The result?

We failed. And, when you fail like this, you damage your reputation. You may never fix it. Or if you do, it's often pretty painful and can take ages.

To succeed first time, the steps are:

- Step 1: Get the meeting.
- Step 2: Prepare. A lot.
- Step 3: Be brilliant during it.

This chapter focuses on the first two – everything *before* the meeting. The next shows what to do *during* it.

Step 1: Get the meeting

Top Dogs are busy. They're often besieged by desperate salespeople under pressure to meet targets and focused on their own agenda.

So, to get a meeting – and for it to be successful – you must differentiate yourself from that lot.

But getting meetings with these Execs is hard. And doing so when they haven't heard of you can be virtually impossible.

But of course, you *have* to be able to do this. If you can't, you might never meet anyone new. That might be ok for the next ten days. But it isn't going to sustain you over the next ten years. There are a number of techniques you could use. Unfortunately, most initially seem daunting (like networking), expensive (advertising) or horrific (cold calling). So choose something that is both:

- Likely to work.
- Pleasant to do.

And, because no business book is complete without a 2x2 matrix, here's how this might look:

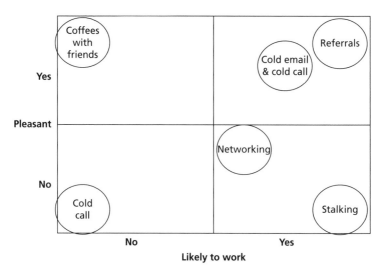

I've used these six blobs to illustrate how the matrix works. Yours would look very different – different blobs; different positions. My rationale for putting these six where they are is:

- Referrals are often best – they're likely to work and pretty pleasant to do.
- Making a cold call *after* you've sent a cold email is also quite likely to work and relatively pleasant. However, cold calling when you *haven't* emailed first works less often. And, let's face it, most people hate doing it.

- The 'coffee with friends' is an important one. Often, it's easy to spend time with people you like – and who like you – but who'll never buy anything. So, yes it's lovely. But it won't lead to business. In fact, the better friends you become, the harder it is to ask them to give you money.
- Networking often works quite well, although lots of people don't like it much.
- Stalking will *definitely* get a meeting. Though it might be pretty unpleasant!

Here's how to get meetings using the best two approaches on my matrix …

Technique 1: Use referrals to get a meeting

Referrals work because, as you know, the business world is powered by personal relationships. One of *your* friends recommending you to one of *theirs* is more compelling than any impersonal marketing campaign could ever be.

And they're pleasant because *everyone* benefits:

- You benefit by getting a warm introduction to a complete stranger quickly, cheaply and painlessly.
- Your referrer friend benefits because he helped two of his friends – you and your target.
- His friend (your target) benefits, because she gets to meet you, share experiences and learn from you.

In fact, there's only one problem with referrals: you don't get enough of them. Your contacts rarely think of referring you. It's not that you don't impress them – far from it. It's just that they don't look at you in that way.

You're the same. Think of the most impressive supplier you know – someone you've used at work or home. How many times – without them asking you to – have you proactively contacted your friends to refer them?

So getting referrals is simply a case of asking for them in the right way. Your words will vary, depending on your relationship with the referrer. But, however you ask, he'll need to know two things from you:

1. Who you want to speak to.
2. Why it's in her interest to speak with you (in other words, examples of AFTERs she'll get from meeting you).

If he doesn't know the former, he won't know who to speak to about you. For example, I once asked a chiropractor who he wanted referrals into. He replied 'anybody with a spine'. Not the clearest steer I've had.

Your referrer also needs to know why it's in his contact's interest to see you. If he doesn't, he'll come across like he's on commission for you ('I want you to speak to my friend Paul') rather than helping his friend ('I want you to speak to my friend Paul, because he can help you achieve AFTER X').

Here are example scripts to trigger referrals. Use them – or something similar – at a time when your contact is feeling positive towards you. Maybe at the end of a contract that went particularly well. The more they feel they owe you, the more likely they are to help.

Example Script	My Script
'Please could you do me a favour?	
I saw on LinkedIn that you know Mrs X.	
I'd love to speak to her, to share experiences about *(topic)*.	
Could you introduce us please?'	
Or...	
'I'm delighted that you're so pleased with the impact we've had in your division.	
I'd love to similarly help Mrs X in Division X. Would you mind introducing us please?'	
Or...	
'Please can I ask your advice?	
You work with lots of corporate lawyers. And I'm keen to get to know more of them, because I can help them with X.	
How would you advise I go about meeting them?	
(If your contact said he'll introduce you, great. If he suggests something else, listen to his advice, and then say ...)	
Thank you – I'll do that. One other idea: which of your lawyer contacts would you feel most comfortable introducing me to?'	

Technique 2: Use cold email/call to get a meeting

As we said earlier, cold calling is hard. But a warm-up email first makes it much easier.

The secret here is to adopt Alpha Dog stance, not subservient Beta. So don't imply 'I know you're so busy and important. Please will you see me? Please? I'll free up my unimportant diary to fit with your important one'.

Instead, Alpha Dog stance means offering value, so she knows meeting you will bring significant gain. Think 'Help. Don't sell'. For example, this script works well:

An invitation to share experiences about [important topic to them]

Dear X,

I am *[insert role describing relevant value – 'I represent company X, specializing in customer acquisition.']*

I've been working extensively in your industry in recent months *[insert relevant topic(s) – 'around the use of data analytics to inform decisions that drive major revenue growth.']*

I would appreciate the opportunity to brief you on some of the trends, challenges and opportunities we've found; and to get your perspective on your company's approach in this area.

(continued)

> With your agreement, I will ask my assistant to contact yours, to arrange a mutually convenient time for us to meet.
>
> I look forward to exchanging views on this important topic.
>
> Kind regards

You'll notice:

- The topic of the meeting is clear, and of use to her.
- The title captures her, so she'll open your email (which is, after all, the only purpose of an email title – to get it opened. Another good reason not to send emails called 'FYI', 'Update', 'RE' or 'Misc') Another title that works well for this email: 'I saw your article in the [press e.g. Times] about [topic].'
- Words like 'brief you' have impact. People usually want to hear what others are doing; and to gain insights that their colleagues don't have.
- You're not directly asking for the meeting. Instead the words 'with your agreement' mean she would have to actively intervene and decline.
- This email uses peer group language, suggesting – not requesting – an exchange of experiences and views. We're Alpha Dogs together.
- You can use this template all the time. Most of it stays the same – you only have to change the three things in italics.
- Because it's your Assistant calling, you don't have to make the call. Result! It's now simply an admin call, rather than a sales one. (If you don't have an Assistant,

make the call yourself remembering *you're only calling to set up the meeting.* Don't discuss anything on the phone or there's no point in her *seeing* you.)

Step 2: Prepare. A lot

You've now got the meeting. To be brilliant *during* it, you must be brilliant *before* it. There are six critical areas:

1. Know who you're meeting.
2. Know her likely challenges.
3. Focus on her AFTERs.
4. Prepare something you'll teach her.
5. Prepare compelling stories.
6. Know your desired outcome from the meeting.

1. Know who you're meeting

It's essential to learn more about her role, past achievements and – if possible – personality (youngish, high achiever, brink of retirement, expressive, analytical, introvert, etc.).

As we discussed earlier, there are many sources of such information – the company website, their accounts, LinkedIn, and so on. If nothing else, at least Google her. If she's worked for other organizations, she may be already known to yours. She may even be an alumni. If this is the case, talk to colleagues to find out as much as you can. (Be careful though: ensure you understand the manner and circumstances of her departure.) Equally, if she's worked for another organization who's a customer of yours, find out your track record with them – both good and bad.

I once met with the Chairman of a power company for whom my company had a number of issues on a project he was sponsoring. I researched all the issues and the actions taken to put them right. Thank goodness I did. It was the first thing he raised after the icebreaker. So it became an icebreaker in itself!

2. Know her likely issues and challenges

If you have targeted a meeting, you'll have some idea of the goods or services you'd like her to buy or sponsor.

So the next step is to understand her agenda and issues, to shape your pitch and avoid the dreaded Product Push. This is where you have a particular service and seek to persuade her she needs it. It can be a viable thing to do, but usually isn't:

Product Push can work when:	It's less effective when:
You know the issues impacting her.	You have a solution looking for an issue.
You know her well enough to bring her new ideas.	You don't know enough about her to know if your product or service relates to her priorities.
The timing is right.	
She hasn't already been sold it by someone else.	You are not the clear, differentiated, market leader.

The opposite is called issues-based selling. This is where her issues lead the discussion:

Issues-based selling works when:	It's less effective when:
You have an interesting point of view about the value you can bring her.	You tell her what the issues are.
You want to demonstrate insight into her business.	You ask for the issues without giving something back and/or before you've built credibility.
You want to start/build a relationship, rather than get 'just' an engagement or transaction.	You tell her what she already knows when she really wanted a new approach.

So if you choose to assume that:

- Your product or service is at the top of her priorities.
- She knows she has a need for it.
- She fully understands that need.
- None of your competitors have offered it already.
- Yours is clearly the superior offering – price or specification or both …

… then Product Push is the way to go. There's plenty of advice available that shows how to do this. In this book though, we focus on issues-based conversations. Those designed to explore her issues, understand their context and build your own credibility before offering solutions. These conversations are designed to establish intimacy and trust. Conversations between equals who are co-developing solutions.

The guiding principles of issues-based selling:

- Deliver value *before* asking for issues and challenges.
- Gain an understanding of her problems and underlying issues.
- Share similar experiences: this sets you up as peers, and helps build genuine mutual engagement and trust.
- Understand what value she attributes to solving her challenges.
- Focus on what you'll leave behind – her AFTERs – not the work you'll do.

---

3. Focus on her AFTERs

In your meeting, it's important you avoid the traditional 'what we do' approach. This is where the 'seller' (you) focuses primarily on your own – not her – agenda. People do this by listing *their own* strengths, *their own* products and services, *their own* thoughts, *their own* specialisms and technology.

Top Dogs don't care. She didn't wake up thinking 'I'd love to know about his unique technology'; she woke up thinking 'how am I going to resolve Issue X?'

Also, it's extraordinarily hard to impress someone about your ability to help them achieve what they want … if you don't know what they want to achieve!

Fortunately for you, the vast majority of your competition will start meetings talking about their own organizations. Does this slide feel depressingly familiar?

About us

- Founded in 1922
- 94 offices throughout the world
- 72,000 staff (plus 7000 part time)
- Strong technical expertise
- Positive growth over past five years
- Committed training office: we have IIP

Start like this, and your buyer sees you as being the same as your competition. It turns her off, not on. She isn't interested in this sort of stuff. Instead, she's only really interested in one of two things:

- More good stuff – more profit, better efficiency, better motivation and morale.
- Less bad stuff – lower risk, less bureaucracy, reduced costs and stress.

In other words, she doesn't want you. She wants the AFTERs of you.

As American Business School Professor Theodore Levitt said: 'People don't want quarter inch drills. They want quarter inch holes'. If you rushed into a DIY store on a Sunday morning, wanting a drill so you could put a mirror up in the spare bedroom, and the Sales Assistant showed you diagrams of how the drill worked – including cogs and gears and everything – it would be pretty annoying. In fact, you might use the drill on him!

In your meetings, focus on her AFTERs – why she'll be better off AFTER working with you. Don't bang on about you and your deliverables. Don't be fixated on slide packs, technical knowledge, and your passion for your thing. This sets up an unsatisfying relationship of seller/buyer. And it means you'll hear one of:

- 'We're doing that already'.
- 'Why do we need you or your product?'
- 'Yes, but our business is different. That won't work here'.
- 'I've heard this before'.

Or my personal favourite – someone told me a buyer had once said 'I'm sorry – but we don't have a problem that fits your solution'. Eek!

Instead, you want to be two Top Dogs sharing experiences and solving challenges. To do this, use the issues-based approach. Focus on building credibility, trust and delivering value. This earns you the right to ask good questions. Her answers to these questions will highlight her key issues. These issues will then drive all your discussions. And you'll keep building her trust in you by:

- Teaching her useful insights she didn't know.
- Using compelling stories – sharing relevant experiences stimulates interest and gets her talking about her challenges.

- Taking time to listen, explore and understand those challenges *before* offering expertise, products and solutions.

4. Prepare something you'll teach her

In Dixon/Adamson's excellent book *The Challenger Sale*, they share the Sales Executive Council's research showing the importance of *challenging* customers. By this, they mean challenging their thinking – helping them see things differently. Teaching them something.

They found this to be the most powerful way to impress a potential customer. There are all sorts of reasons for this:

- When you say something that makes people think 'I'd never thought of it like that', they see you as value-adding. Normally, they have to wait until after they've paid money before they get value like this.
- It differentiates you. Since you've taught them something new, they can't have heard it from anyone else.
- They're more likely to want to see you again – 'what else can he teach me?'
- The problem with 'only' asking questions to uncover issues is that she might not know what's best for her. There'll be lots of things she doesn't know she doesn't know. In fact, when you think about it, how can *she* possibly know as much as *you* about *your* area of expertise? My favourite quote about this: Henry Ford – *'If I'd done what my customers wanted, I would have built a faster horse'*.

There are many ways to find things you can teach her. For example, think which parts of your expertise are most relevant to her. You're bound to know something she doesn't (if you don't, that's a big problem!).

Or look at your WWF stories – see the next section for how to write those – and ask yourself 'how can I turn my micro story into a macro teaching point?' In other words, how can you use your learnings with other companies to give her useful advice?

Or call one or two of her main stakeholders – customers, employees etc. – and ask them for their insights that you can share with her.

Or Google her, her company, and her competitors.

Or go to one of the business research sites and find relevant stats.

Or ask your colleagues for ideas.

Or ask subject matter experts.

There are *loads* of sources. Use them to take something that makes her think 'I'd never thought of it like that'. You'll both be grateful you did.

5. Prepare compelling stories

Many people prove their credentials by explaining how they go about their business.

But this just proves what they *do*; not that it *works*.

That's like me saying I'm going to explain my five-step approach for getting a date on a Friday night. But then, after I've run through them, you asking 'and have you actually ever had a date on a Friday night using this approach?'

To which I reply 'Er, not as such. No'.

> **Facts tell. Stories sell.**

Telling stories is a much better approach. They're more interesting, memorable and differentiating – after all, nobody else can use *your* stories (even better, your competitors are probably still banging on about their products and services anyway).

Best of all: they prove your stuff works. For example, if I told you a *story* about a successful date I had last Friday, you'd know my five steps worked – and quite possibly be desperate to know what they were!

Good stories stimulate the sort of interaction you want – two Top Dogs having a two-way, valuable discussion.

Your stories should:

- Be interesting.
- Be succinct with relevant points: less is more – about 100 words.
- Build curiosity.
- Directly address her issues …
- … and raise some more.
- Be rehearsed, but 'spontaneous'.
- Contain multiple points.

A good technique is 'What We Found' (WWF). This is where you tell of the work you did for someone else, but do so in reverse, leading with the AFTERs:

Set-up

- So Mrs Buyer, you want AFTER X?

Story

- We've done it before, helping CUSTOMER NAME achieve AFTER X.
- Like you, they had a problem with Y.
- So what we did for them was Z.

This sounds easy enough. But when I teach people this technique, I consistently encounter the fear that they don't have any good stories. I've asked many audiences to volunteer something good they've done for their customers. Nobody ever does.

I've discovered the reason is because people focus on what they *do* (the deliverables), not what they *cause* (the AFTERs). So they can't really describe 'what we found' because they didn't find any AFTERs. Here's a conversation from a recent workshop:

Me: Who has achieved a great outcome for a customer?
Participants: [Stunned silence]
Me: Come on. *Someone* must have.
Participant: [Eventually] I did.
Me: Great, who was the customer?
Participant: X plc.

Me: No, what was the name of your actual *customer*? And their role?

Participant: Steve X. He was the CIO.

Me: And what value did you deliver to Steve?

Participant: We got involved when they sold their core business along with their IT infrastructure.

Me: No. That's what you *did*. What value did you deliver? In other words, why was he better off *after* you'd finished?

Participant: His previous set-up was going to waste £hundreds-of-millions. We stopped that happening.

Me: Great! Now we're getting somewhere. And why was that important?

Participant: He wanted a global best-in-class team; and we were able to deliver one.

Me: And now let's work backwards and fill in some missing details – the who, when, where, how, and so on …

The dialogue continued like this for a while. We eventually established he'd addressed a critical business issue, added huge value and delivered something truly distinctive.

His WWF became:

'We recently worked with the CIO of X plc – a guy called Steve X.

We saved him £hundreds-of-millions by structuring his IT, so it gave him a huge competitive advantage in their market.

What had happened was this: his company had divested their core underperforming business, and Steve had to help build the new business very quickly. Delay in doing so would cost £millions every month.

His big issue was that the IT infrastructure had gone with the divestment. He needed the replacement built quickly and with complete reliability. In addition, he needed to train his people with new skills, and develop new approaches to analysing data.

We delivered the fastest, most effective (brand-name IT system) implementation in history – resulting in the new business launching ahead of schedule, delivering in excess of £100 million in value.

We're now helping Steve use the system to analyse data in a way that produces better insight than his competitors.'

How amazing is *that*?

Much better than his first answer – stunned silence.

And his second – *'We got involved when they sold their core business along with their IT infrastructure.'*

This guy had delivered massive value. But he didn't see it for what it was. Nor did his firm. So nobody used it when trying to impress new Top Dogs!

You too could be missing some amazing WWF stories. Here's how to find, then write, them:

- Think of a recent large project you worked on.
- Understand the challenges that led your customer to need your products or services.

- List the top-level deliverables of your project – what you *did*.
- Establish the value you delivered – why they were better off AFTERwards – what you *caused*. As discussed before, this could be more good stuff (like profits) and/ or less bad (reduced costs).
- Create a personalized compelling story around them, using the work-backwards approach from before:

Set-up

- So Mrs Buyer, you want AFTER X?

Story

- We've done it before, helping CUSTOMER NAME achieve AFTER X.
- Like you, they had a problem with Y.
- So what we did for them was Z.

In summary, you clearly distinguish yourself from competitors by creating:

- Intimacy – through storytelling, sharing confidences (without breaching ethics around confidentiality), alluding to peers in an intimate way, and so on.
- Credibility – through discussing her issues first, then the results she wants, but *not* your product or method of delivery (yet). You also appear lower risk when it's clear you've helped similar companies with similar issues.

6. Know your desired outcome from the meeting

> 'If you don't know where you are going,
> any road will take you there'.
>
> *George Harrison*

It's surprising how many people set up a meeting without first determining their desired outcome.

If you don't do this *before* the meeting, how do you know it's worth having?

If you don't review this *after* it, how do you know it worked?

Even more surprising: many meetings don't start by attendees agreeing the desired outcome. But this means you and she aren't necessarily aiming for the same things. This results in the all-too-common phenomenon of all meetings being great:

> Me: How did yesterday's meeting go with the Exec?
> Colleague: Great.
> Me: Brilliant. Why? What was the result?
> Colleague: Well, we'd only booked an hour. But she gave us an hour and 20 minutes. She told us all about what she was doing and all the successes she's had.
> Me: Er – OK. And is there any follow-up?
> Colleague: Yes. She said she had nothing for us at the moment. But asked us to call again in a few months' time.

Now that to me is NOT a great meeting. In fact, it's a rubbish one. My colleague overran his allotted time –

quite possibly creating chaos in a busy person's diary. He didn't unearth any new issues or challenges. There were no follow-up actions. All that happened was the target had a great time having a captive audience to whom she could big herself up.

A great meeting delivers your desired outcome, such that all parties are engaged with it.

That's so important, it's worth repeating:

> **A great meeting delivers your desired outcome, such that all parties are engaged with it.**

This desired outcome might be:

- A follow-up meeting to further develop potential solutions to her issues.
- Introductions to other key people in her organization.
- To test a hypothesis.
- To qualify a potential sale.
- To secure her sponsorship to 'unstick' a conversation that isn't progressing quickly with her subordinates …

… whatever it is, you should know your success criteria *before* you go in.

And, once you do, it's 'just' a case of achieving this success by delivering a great meeting. Chapter 5 shows the best way to do so.

Doggie Treats

Get – then prepare for – a great first meeting

- Top Dogs are busy. They'll only find time for meetings that bring them value. Ensure yours do.
- Beware: a monologue about your company's history and services – accompanied by a detailed slide deck no doubt – brings no value to her. Unless she wanted to know about that. And nothing else. Which she didn't. Discuss this in your first meeting, and you're less likely to get a second one.
- Book the meeting by using techniques that are both likely to work and pleasant to do. For example, more referrals and less cold calls.
- People rarely refer you unless you ask them to. So ask.
- If you do want to cold call, send a warm-up email first.
- Prepare brilliantly:
  - Know who you're meeting – do some research.
  - Know her likely challenges – think issues-based, not Product Push.
  - Focus on her AFTERs, not your deliverables.
  - Prepare something you'll teach her, so she thinks 'I'd never thought of it like that'.
  - Prepare compelling stories – 'Facts tell; stories sell'.
  - Know your desired outcomes from the meeting, or you won't get them.

5

Walkies!

Deliver a great first meeting

When I train my dogs, there are some rules for keeping them engaged:

- Know my desired outcome.
- Have a plan for how to achieve it …
- … but be flexible, and adapt to their moods.
- Make it fun.
- Keep it interesting.
- Always be present-focused, alert and observe their body language.
- Be patient.
- Finish while they're still keen.

A pretty good blueprint for your next meeting, yes?

And, with dogs (though not humans!), I train them while they're hungry. They're more alert then. Though, as the session progresses, they become increasingly distracted by their next event – a bowl of delicious dry biscuits. So I end the session early.

This also applies to meetings with busy Executives – although they might be more distracted by their next meeting, rather than dog biscuits. Depends on the meeting, I guess.

So when meeting with Executives, you have to wow them quickly, and then get out of their way so they can go to their next meeting/biscuits. Fortunately, most of your competitors can't do this. More good news; there are only six steps to master:

1. Establish rhythm.
2. Start well, using your icebreaker.
3. Transition from icebreaker to agenda.
4. Share experiences and add value to each other:
    • she goes first; or
    • you go first.
5. Keep being an Alpha Dog (don't be subordinated).
6. Confirm next steps.

1. Establish rhythm

It's easy to talk too much. Especially when you're nervous.

Annoyingly, it's also easy to talk too little, and become a nod-along Beta Dog. Especially when an Executive uses your meeting to expand on her achievements.

Neither approach works. One of you bores or frustrates the other.

So it's best to have a broad plan as to how you want the meeting to run. By that, I mean know *who* you expect to be talking to, about *what*, and *when*. For example, early on,

I want the Executive to be speaking approximately 80% of the time. Not 50%. And certainly not 0%. I can then use this as a way of timing my interventions and retaining control of the meeting.

Meeting stages and rhythm

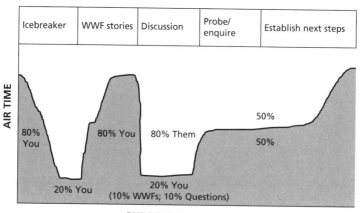

Icebreaker	WWF stories	Discussion	Probe/ enquire	Establish next steps

AIR TIME

80% You

80% You

80% Them

50%

50%

20% You

20% You
(10% WWFs; 10% Questions)

BUILDING ENGAGEMENT

KEY: Them
You

2. Start well, using your icebreaker

Start with your pre-prepared icebreaker. After all, it breaks the ice!

As we discussed earlier, this should quickly lead to a peer-to-peer exchange as you build rapport.

Take care though not to allow the social chat to extend too long, or you'll waste the energy/time you need for the next part. You don't want your meeting to turn into an hour-long icebreaker.

3. Transition from icebreaker to agenda

At the appropriate time – usually within a few minutes – intervene and transition to the business part of the meeting.

This is easiest when you know *in advance* what words you're going to say. If you don't, the words might not come to you when it matters. And if you don't know what to say, you won't say anything. So the chit-chat will meander on. And on. And on.

Here's an example script that works well. If it sounds like you, use it. If not, choose another:

Example script	My script
'Jane, the purpose of our meeting is for us to share experiences and compare views about [topic]. How would you like us to do this? I can start with some accounts of what we've found with other customers. Or you could start and talk about your own particular situation here at X. Which would you prefer?'	

4. Share experiences and add value to each other

You're now into the meat of the meeting.

And you've arrived here as *peers*. You've built some rapport. You've both contributed. And, trust me, she is *not* thinking 'This is all very well. But what year were you founded?'

For the next part, it's important you *both* learn and *both* add value to each other. You achieve this by sharing experiences. She'll tell you about her situation, issues and priorities. You'll provide interesting value with your pre-prepared WWF stories.

There are only two ways this part of the meeting will go. Either she goes first, or you do. Done properly, both work. The first is better in that you uncover her priorities *before* telling your WWFs. This helps you tailor your stories to her situation. The second is better in that you deliver value early, by teaching her things she didn't know.

Let's start by looking at when she chooses to share first …

Option 1: She goes first

She'll begin by explaining why she was interested in seeing you. Her reasons will probably be because she wants to know more about the issue you outlined in your pre-meeting communications. It must have resonated with her, or she wouldn't be meeting you.

While she's speaking, you need to exercise that very rare skill – rarer than hens' teeth in a salesperson – the ability to shut up and listen.

Although you might find this difficult, remember that your less talented competitors tend to lose the plot here. They see her words as the chance they've been craving to demonstrate their deep technical expertise. They'll leap in, discussing their approaches, methods and products. Pre-prepared slide packs will be slammed down and talked through at length. The meeting will become a sales presentation. An undifferentiated, obvious, tedious sales presentation. Not the exchange of experiences and insights between equals that you're looking for. And she'll probably hate it.

Instead, explore why what she's said is of interest to her. Delve further into her agenda and issues. After all, this was what you arranged the meeting to do. Ask probing questions, offering occasional insight based on your experience. You should *not* at this stage offer solutions. Nobody wants experts to give solutions too early. I certainly don't want my doctor prescribing a drug before she knows what's wrong with me.

Good probing questions include:

- Please could you tell me more about that?
- What was the impact of that decision on your business?

- What was the impact on *you*?
- What happened next?

It's sensible to have a few go-to questions like this that you trot out in most meetings. So choose your favourites and use them whenever appropriate. Remember: she won't know which questions you ask in other meetings. So if certain ones work, keep using them (and avoid the issue you find in so many businesses: 'it worked so well, we never did it again').

As she continues to talk, you want the conversation to progress towards a discussion about the size of the prize – the value she'd gain from successfully tackling the issue. The more valuable she perceives this to be; the more likely it is to happen. You also want to assess where these challenges sit on her agenda:

- How important is this issue to you?
- Where does it sit on your list of priorities?
- Why is this issue so important to you?
- What is the driver behind addressing this issue? Cost? Revenue? Risk? All of these? Something else?
- What is the business case for doing something about it?
- How will you measure success?
- How will your boss measure it?
- What barriers are you finding to addressing it?
- How time critical is it? Why? What's the cost of delay?

The key is to identify whether this is her most important issue, rather than a topic she latched onto because it happened to be mentioned in your earlier conversations.

Once her answers suggest you're hitting on significant priorities, continue to probe. Let her run with it for a while. It's oh-so-tempting – where her first issue is one you've met before and have a solution for – to rush in and demonstrate your knowledge and expertise too early. But providing solutions now makes her think you're 'just another salesperson'. And/or you'll fail to discover further insight and opportunities. Neither is good.

Oh, and one more thing: Put. The. Slides. Away.

The final area to uncover about her key issues is her progress so far:

- What initiatives are under way to address the issue?
- How much progress have you made so far in addressing it?

Think OMG!

You'll know you have a good grasp of her key priorities if you know her OMG:

- **O**bjectives – what she wants to achieve.
- **M**easures – how she'll know she's achieved them.
- **G**ain – the value to her in achieving them.

- What challenges have you found in addressing it?

Although she's done most of the talking so far, you've delivered lots of value by helping clarify her OMG. This helps differentiate you from the competition – after all, they didn't provide this clarity. They did however provide a wonderful slide deck.

And, as we discussed in earlier chapters, you can also deliver value by *teaching* her useful insights about these priority areas. Remember, you want her to think 'well, I'd never thought of it like that'. The best way to do this is by using your pre-prepared WWF stories. They'll include new ideas and insights that will develop her thinking.

To bridge across to these WWFs – rather than with a clunky 'STORY ALERT – LISTEN TO THE THING I'VE PREPARED' – know how you'll introduce it, and what you'll say to end it. For example:

Intro: transition to your WWF	
Example script	**My script**
'Your situation reminds me of a similar project I worked on at X plc ...'	
Outro: transition out, and get her talking again	
Example script	**My script**
'Would you like to know more about what I learned on this project?' Or 'Does that resonate with your situation?'	

Because she discussed her issues *before* your WWF, you probably managed to choose a story that *did* resonate. So she'll want to learn more. She'll probably ask questions like 'how did you do that?'

A great response here: 'I can bring the team of experts who did the work to talk you through it in depth. But, before we do that, what's behind your question?'

Then pause, look interested and expectant – in Labrador terms, ears cocked forward and your head slightly on one side. She'll reply, and now you're back to talking about her issues, why they're critical and how her life will be better once they're resolved.

Option 2: You go first

The alternative approach – where you tell your stories *before* asking about hers – also works well. Because you teach – so, add value – early.

The downside of going first is you don't know enough about her priorities. So there's a greater chance your first WWF story won't be 100% relevant. So here's what you do if she wants you to go first …

Start with your best, most relevant WWF. Introduce it by referring to your previous conversations

If your story resonates, she'll say 'how did you do that?' Then, as above, you say 'what's behind your question?' and you're talking about her issues. Happy days. You'll then use the

OMG approach/questions to uncover the areas discussed in the previous section.

Example script	My script
'When we spoke last week, you mentioned (topic) X, and your desire to cause (AFTERs) Y. We've done similar work with (company) Z. What happened was ...' (story)	

If however Story One *doesn't* resonate, tell a second one on a different topic. If it causes a better reaction, you're off and running. If not, don't panic. Simply re-group and change tactic. You've shared some experiences. This earns you the right to get her talking, by asking:

Example script	My script
'I don't know if any of these experiences have resonated with you? Rather than have me talk at you further, it would be interesting to hear about your current challenges'.	

Either she'll say that some of your WWFs *do* resonate, and why. Or she'll begin to talk about her most significant challenges. Either way, you're back on track!

One important final note: take as long as you want on this part of the meeting. But make sure you end it 10–15 minutes before the scheduled finish time – to allow for confirming next steps.

5. Keep being an Alpha Dog (don't be subordinated)

A logical conclusion to the meeting would be that she expresses real interest and suggests further meetings with her colleagues – hopefully with a warm introduction from her – who are key stakeholders of your project.

This can feel like victory for you. After all, she must be interested – she's sending you to speak to colleagues. And if you do meet with them – as opposed to sending your colleagues to do so – there are benefits in that you:

- Continue the threads from your meeting with her.
- Don't have to trust your colleagues to deliver great meetings for you.
- Retain full control of the process.
- Can claim sole credit when it goes well!

So, yes it can feel like a good outcome.

But it isn't. Far from it.

In fact, there's a big heffalump trap to avoid here. When you meet with her juniors, it's easy to become subordinated. In other words, everyone thinks of you as *their* peer, not *hers*. And, once there, it's hard to climb back up to her level again. So, while it's true that seeing her subordinates might deliver a short-term sale, it won't help sustain a long-term, peer-level relationship with the Top Dog.

Worse, her subordinates may be highly resistant to your solution, because they:

- Feel they own the challenge, so you're treading on their turf.
- Perceive inherent criticism that their boss has sent you to them.
- Might associate you with this criticism: in fact, they might think you're the cause of it – 'we were fine till you showed up'.
- Might already have a preferred provider of your solution.
- Think their own position, role or even livelihood could be threatened by your solution.

The easiest way for them to see you off would be to appear amiable, smile, nod along … and then go to their boss and give her 100 reasons why you're wrong, too expensive or that they have it under control … Whatever the real reason, there's a strong risk you'll never hear it.

So, when she asks you to meet her juniors, simply say: 'by all means, I will get my team to connect with them. Once they've done so, you and I should re-group to digest how those meetings went'.

You then send a colleague – well briefed and rehearsed, of course – to the subordinate meeting. This means you remain Alpha Dog.

Plus, because you've agreed upfront that you'll meet her later to discuss their meeting, you can manage change resistance more effectively. For example, if their meeting went badly, you can suggest there might have been poor chemistry between your and her colleagues. You can say something like 'If chemistry is the issue, we can of course change the team. But before we do that, do you think there may be resistance for other reasons that we should explore?'

This should result in a peer discussion about why people might be resistant, and how you both can manage that obstacle. Whereas, if you'd been at that junior meeting, it's harder to manage this type of scenario. You may be the subject of criticism. Some may stick.

A final point about these subordinate meetings: set them up for success by using the right introduction. If the Executive sets them up badly, you'll be perceived as being foisted on them by their boss. You become a threat to their position in their own pack.

Therefore, suggest that the Executive doesn't send a communication leading with you and your organization. Instead, ask for one that focuses on the business benefits first. Look at these two example emails. If you were her junior, which would be better?

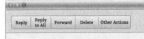

Email example 1

Subject: Please meet with Company X

Peter, I have been discussing using Company X to sort out our current IT challenge. I have asked them to set up a meeting with you to get your views. They will be in touch shortly.

Kind regards

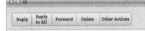

Email example 2

Subject: Some new thoughts about helping our sales force drive more sales

Peter,

I have been giving a lot of thought to our discussions around the challenge of getting the right insight and information to our sales force, to focus their efforts and drive more sales.

I want to put this right to the top of our priorities.

> I have had an interesting discussion with company X recently. And, while I have made no decision to do anything with them, they have some interesting perspectives.
>
> I have suggested they would benefit from sharing experiences with you, and they will be in touch shortly.
>
> Let's meet to discuss how best to progress once you have met them.
>
> Kind regards

As a recipient, which would you be less resistant to?

6. Confirm next steps

You're in a great place now. You've captured her interest. You've established personal and professional credibility. You've gained real insight into her most important challenges. You've told her impressive stories. You've taught her useful stuff. You might even have started to explore how your products and services could help.

What else could there be?

Well, only the most important thing.

To arrange a second meeting. Without it, your first meeting becomes a total waste of time. (By the way, *don't* seek to close a sale now. It's unlikely to happen. It's far more likely to undo all your good work by suddenly positioning yourself as just another salesperson.)

Example script	My script
'I'm conscious of time. I suggest we meet again to continue our dialogue. (if appropriate) I also suggest that I bring (name), one of my colleagues with a lot of experience in this area to share his views also. In the meantime, can I suggest you think about the specific areas that you would like to focus on, to ensure we have a really useful second meeting? For example: • Some more thoughts on how you'd measure success. • Likely barriers we'll need to overcome. • The factors that would make the biggest difference to you – accelerated timescales, a clearer definition of value, less risk, and so on'.	

Assuming agreement, just say you'll arrange something in the near future. Shake hands. And get out.

Two final points – both important enough to have their own box:

#1 'Thank you' is not peer group language

When Misty and Elsa want to show they recognize Brook is the Alpha Dog, they lick her under the chin. This is typical pack behaviour observed over thousands of years by their wolf ancestors.

If you end your meeting by thanking the Executive for her time – or worse, for *sparing* it to meet with you – you may just as well lick her under her chin!

Alpha Dog stance – the language of equals – requires you only to say 'I enjoyed our meeting and will be in touch soon'.

#2 Never, ever finish late. Ever.

There are few (no?) more valuable commodities in a busy Executive's day than time.

Tempting as it is when the conversation is flowing, overrunning is almost always a bad thing to do:

- If you don't end the meeting, she will. Alpha Dogs draw meetings to a close.
- If you overrun, you're encroaching on her schedule. This may irritate and/or cause stress in her day – not the impression you want to give.
- You must leave her wanting more.

Even when in full flow and with energy levels high, end the meeting early. This helps ensure she agrees to the all-important second one. The next chapter explains how best to wow her when you go back.

Doggie Treats

Deliver a great first meeting

- Pre-plan the meeting's rhythm – know *who* you want to be speaking to, about *what*, and *when*. If you don't, it's harder to know whether it's going well/badly.
- Use pre-prepared scripts to impress and inject pace. For example, your icebreakers, transitions and probing questions.
- Use your WWF stories to add value, insights and certainty you can help her.
- Don't allow yourself to be subordinated.
- Don't say 'thank you for sparing your time'.
- Don't finish late, even if things are going well.
- Allow time to agree next steps. You don't want to rush this. It's the most important bit.

6

Keep walking!

Build momentum in subsequent meetings

Misty loves dribbling a football round our garden. She does it for hours.

But when someone appears on the driveway, it's game over. She deserts the ball and runs to greet them. She rarely then returns to the ball. In fact, she's forgotten all about it. The distraction proved too distracting.

Becoming distracted doesn't just happen to her, of course. Have *you* ever lost track of a conversation mid-flow? Forgotten what you were going to say? I know I have.

Busy Executives are the same. No matter how compelling your meeting was, within a few hours, she'll have had many other distractions – crises, challenges, meetings … not to mention actually doing her day job.

Your meeting won't stay at the top of her mind. It just won't. Not your fault. Not hers. It's the way it is.

You, however, will be the opposite. You'll have written up meeting notes – probably in lots of detail. You'll have discussed them with colleagues. You'll have started pulling together information for her. Maybe created a couple of documents. Maybe even told your boss how well the meeting went.

In short: the meeting – and the opportunity it represents – stays higher on your list of priorities than it does on hers. So, it's imperative you work hard to stay a priority to her – both *before* and *during* Meeting Two.

Prepare impressive follow-up communications

One simple way to stay on her radar: send two short emails:

1. One immediately after Meeting One.
2. One immediately before Meeting Two.

Email One is simply confirmation of next steps. For example:

> **Looking forward to our next meeting on [DATE]**
>
> Jane,
>
> I enjoyed our meeting yesterday.
>
> As promised, I'll [list your main actions].
>
> I look forward to sharing these with you on [date], and to hearing about [her actions].
>
> Regards,
>
> John

There's no new content in this email, nor should there be. It's more of a reminder about what you agreed. Also, of course, people tend to reply to emails like this – it's always nice to get an 'I enjoyed it too' message back.

A few days before Meeting Two, send Email Two – something like:

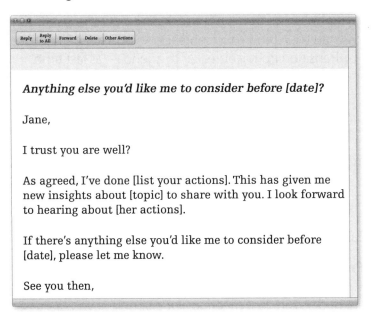

Reply | Reply to All | Forward | Delete | Other Actions

Anything else you'd like me to consider before [date]?

Jane,

I trust you are well?

As agreed, I've done [list your actions]. This has given me new insights about [topic] to share with you. I look forward to hearing about [her actions].

If there's anything else you'd like me to consider before [date], please let me know.

See you then,

How to prepare for second and subsequent meetings

Meeting One had six steps (see Chapter 5):

1. Establish rhythm.
2. Start well using your icebreaker.

3. Transition from icebreaker to agenda.
4. Share experiences and add value to each other – using WWFs and probing questions.
5. Keep being an Alpha Dog – don't be subordinated.
6. Confirm next steps.

For Meeting Two, it's the same, but with a few tweaks:

- Establish rhythm – not needed. You did this last time.
- Start well using your icebreaker – you'll need a new one.
- Transition from icebreaker to agenda – as last time.
- Share experiences and add value to each other – you'll need new WWF stories.
- Keep being an Alpha Dog – as last time.
- Confirm next steps – as last time.

Your prep for this meeting will also contain two new areas:

- Start shaping the solution for her.
- Decide whether to bring colleagues with you.

Taking each in turn …

Prepare a second icebreaker
This should be easy to write. Simply build on what you learned at your first meeting. For example, if you discussed an approaching holiday, family event or such like, use that. Ask how it went. All the rules of the first icebreaker apply; but continuity is important.

Prepare to transition from icebreaker to agenda
Remember how I said that people often forget what they've just heard? (I guess it'd be ironic if you've forgotten!) Well,

assume she doesn't remember your first meeting as vividly as you do. So remind her and warm her up:

Example script	My script
'Jane, when we last met, you shared a number of challenges about topic X, which we discussed.	
I said I'd go back and look at our experiences in successfully addressing these issues, to share with you today.	
(Where appropriate) Also, I brought *(name)* along, because he's delivered significant results to a number of your competitors addressing these issues.	
For example, when we worked with Emma the CFO at X plc, her challenge was similar to yours *(start your first WWF)*'.	

Prepare new WWFs

Meeting One developed your thinking about how your products and services might deliver value to her. But don't leap straight to these in Meeting Two. It's too sales-y.

Instead, develop more WWFs that relate directly to the issues she raised in Meeting One. As before, these new

WWFs must demonstrate your expertise in having delivered tangible results when working with other customers on similar issues.

Now, it might be that your organization doesn't immediately appear to have credentials that directly mirror her issues. But there'll be something relevant somewhere. So look hard. Ask around. Then bring them together into two or three WWFs, using the 'work backwards' technique from earlier.

Begin to shape the solution
You'll also want to develop initial ideas as to how your products and services fit her needs. After all, you're hoping she wants to discuss this with you one day.

Be careful though: you won't be presenting a fully architected solution yet – even if you secretly create it in advance. Don't undo all your hard work by slipping into full-on Sales Mode and banging on about how you can help – no matter how exciting the opportunity.

Instead, make sure you have at least an outline plan that you can discuss with her. And remember: sketching a solution 'live' is more impressive, compelling and memorable than presenting a pre-prepared slide-set.

Consider bringing other attendees
Although your first meeting was one-to-one, this is the time to consider bringing other experts with you, to share their insights. Of course, you could continue the conversation one-to-one if you want. But only after a thorough briefing,

and armed with knowledge and stories co-created by expert colleagues.

Step 2 – Impress during Meeting Two

The meeting starts as you'd expect, using your pre-prepared content:

- Your icebreaker kicks things off.
- Your transition moves you smoothly into the juicy part of the meeting.
- Your WWFs/her new thoughts dig deeper and draw you closer together.

For the rest of the meeting, you'll:

- Co-develop the solution:
  - #1: Paint a picture of the future.
  - #2: Work backwards to show how you'll get there.
  - #3: Write a timeline.
- Identify potential obstacles, and how to remove them.
- Keep being her Alpha Dog, making sure you aren't subordinated.
- Agree next steps.

Co-develop the solution

A basic tenet of human nature: people tend not to resist ideas they helped create.

So it's important to co-create her solution *with* her, rather than just present one *at* her. As always, do this by starting in the future and working backwards. In effect, putting the AFTERs *before* everything else. This starts to create a picture of you working together, and associates doing so with tangible success.

#1: Paint a picture of the future

Start by (re)confirming her AFTERs. Use OMG to help – Objectives, Measures, Gains. You'll have some idea of these from Meeting One. So either:

- Start here ('Last time, you said X') and then add to it ('Does this cover everything you want? What's missing?')
- Ask –'Jane, imagine we're sitting here in one year's time, meeting to celebrate success, what would it look like? How would success be measured? What might we have done together?'

#2: Work backwards to show how you'll get there

Once you've agreed this attractive vision of the future together, work backwards to identify how best to get there.

Start by asking her views – 'I have some thoughts on how we might achieve this. But I'd love to hear yours first?'

Chip in ideas, using your secretly-pre-prepared solution. But make sure you let her keep talking. Don't be too dogmatic. Also, don't get too carried away and slip into Sales Mode. Check constantly for comfort and input from her. It's a strong indicator of success when you're both fighting for the whiteboard pen.

Also, use the language of mutual qualification to further differentiate you from her alternatives. In a peer-level relationship, you'll both be qualifying whether you can deliver the AFTERs together. A good technique is to regularly use the word 'if' – 'if we were to do this, then …'.

'If' is peer group language. Saying 'we could' and 'we can' is Beta Dog salesperson talking. People are often surprised when I tell them this. But it's a good technique. By saying 'if', you're demonstrating that – while she may be evaluating you – at the same time, you're evaluating her and the potential opportunity. In other words, you'd only work with her if you're convinced you can deliver AFTERs together.

During this phase, you both contribute ideas to ensure you've covered everything. A good question to keep asking is 'If we only did what we've discussed so far, would it deliver our outcomes? Or is something missing?'

#3: Write a timeline
When you're finished chatting, a timeline is a useful output from your co-creation discussions. It clearly shows who's doing what, when.

Although your discussion might have required a lot of thought and input, creating the timeline won't. It's simply a visual summary of your discussions. So it's pretty easy to do; and is a quick way of ensuring you're aligned. Timelines can be simple or complex, depending on the project. Here's a simple example to illustrate what you're looking for:

How we'll increase sales through better negotiating

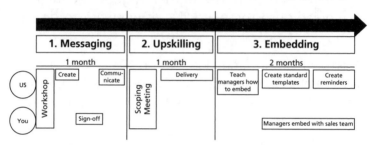

You'll notice:

- Her AFTERs are in the title, to remind her where you're taking her.
- Once she sees this – especially since she's helped create it – you're in a great position to progress your discussion quickly and smoothly.
- Having a row for each of you clearly shows that you're working *together* to deliver her AFTERs.
- She'll enjoy seeing you have lots of actions in your row; and that she doesn't have many in hers!
- Finally, because you *jointly* created it, it sets the tone for the next part of the conversation: *jointly* identifying obstacles and how to remove them.

Identify potential obstacles, and how to remove them

You're now in a good place. You've both agreed what she's looking to achieve, how she'll know she's achieved it, and the value to her in doing so. You also have a visual showing the key phases of the project.

The next step is to identify obstacles you might encounter, and how to avoid them happening. (Again, note how impressive and differentiating this is. By now, many people would be running out of her office, waving their timeline about and jumping for joy. But you aren't. You're more 'real' than this. You know there'll be challenges that could derail you. And you know it's essential they're discussed early.)

Identifying obstacles is a combination of prompting – 'when we've run similar projects before, X has been a problem. Might we experience something similar?' – and asking her. Good questions include:

- Why might this *not* work?
- What are the biggest obstacles we might encounter?
- What might get in the way?
- Who are the main stakeholders in this? Who would support and who might resist? What would lie behind that resistance?

Confirm next steps

As always, you'll end with agreeing next steps.

Depending on your progress so far, this will either be:

- Further meetings – in which case, this chapter is relevant again.
- Submitting some form of proposal – described in the next chapter.

Either way, remember: the aim of any meeting is that something happens after it. So make sure you come out with clear, agreed actions so you can move things forward.

Doggie Treats

Build momentum in subsequent meetings

- Impressive follow-up emails – written in Alpha Dog language – help you stay on her radar.
- Meeting Two requires similar prep to Meeting One – icebreakers, WWFs etc. – though much of it is easier because you now know more about her and her issues.
- Begin to shape a solution – but don't give lots of detail (yet).
- Bring other colleagues if their expertise will help.
- A key output from Meeting Two: a co-created solution – start with their AFTERs, then work backwards until you have a timeline showing what needs to happen, when.
- Find, then remove, likely obstacles.
- As always, confirm next steps – Meeting Three or a proposal.

7

Become Top Dog (1)

Write a compelling proposal/business case

When you've finished all your discussions, it's time to put your proposal in writing. The ideal here, of course: she reads it, loves it and says 'Yes. That's brilliant. Start'.

In many ways, proposal-writing should be the easiest step of all. After all, you've done all the hard work, in that you:

- Managed to get a meeting with a busy Executive – a total stranger.
- Built great rapport with her.
- Impressed her enough at Meeting One so she'd see you again.
- Overcame her objections.
- Overcame your nerves.
- Co-created a solution you're both happy with.

It's an impressive list! Now, you 'only' need to write down what you've agreed, such that she gives you the go-ahead.

Easy, yes?

Well, in theory maybe. But there's more pain associated with proposals than virtually any other sales activity. For example, do you recognize thinking any of these?

- 'Proposals take ages to write'.
- 'And they're really boring to write'.
- 'I'm sure customers are bored reading them'.
- 'Or they don't even read parts/any of them'.
- 'They only care about the price. I don't know why I'm writing anything else'.
- 'I'm never quite sure what to put in there'.
- 'Often, I send them, and never hear back'.
- 'Hand on heart, I don't know the best way to write a good one'.
- 'I have lots of proposals out right now. I can't seem to close any of them'.
- 'I. Just. Hate. Them'.

It doesn't need to be like this! In fact, it mustn't be. Whatever your motivation for doing the job you do, it *isn't* to spend ages doing something you hate, that you don't think will even be read, let alone achieve what you want it to.

Quick answers to the most common proposal problems

Here are some quick answers to these complaints. They provide a good scene-set for the rest of the chapter.

Complaint	Solution
Proposals take ages to write.	• Before putting pen to paper, agree with the customer what content she wants in there. Believe me, this is much quicker – and more accurate – than guessing.
And they're really boring to write.	• However, there will be certain content you want to include in every proposal. So, create standard chunks, for you to cut/paste – with tweaks – into each new one (checking first with her if she'd find them useful).
I'm sure customers are bored reading them. Or they don't even read parts/any of them.	• Since you've asked the customer what she wants in the proposal, she's more likely to read it.
They only care about the price. I don't know why I'm writing anything else.	• So why not just send her a one-line email saying 'It's £125,000. Yes or no?' • Of course she wants more info than this. The trick is to find out what it is.
I'm never quite sure what to put in there.	• So ask her.
Often, I send them, and never hear back.	• Agree *in advance of sending the proposal* when you'll speak again after she's received it.
Hand on heart, I don't know the best way to write a good one.	• This chapter will show you what to do.

(continued)

Complaint	Solution
I have lots of proposals out right now. I can't seem to close any of them.	• Contact them all – using whichever channel is best for each prospect (email, text, chat etc.) – and close them down.
I. Just. Hate. Them.	• Do everything in this chapter, and you won't any more.

Here's more detail on the right-hand column ...

Send the proposal late

By 'late', I don't mean miss your deadline.

I mean send it right at the end – after *all* your discussions.

You want your proposal to confirm what you've already agreed. A good test: you should be able to write 'as agreed' before every sentence. You won't write this of course – it might get a tad boring – but in theory you should be able to.

Now, if you're like most people, as you read the above two paragraphs, you're probably thinking 'I don't do that at the minute. I send them earlier. Why should I change?'

The answer is simply this: your best salesperson is you – not a piece of paper. If your proposal contains new stuff, you're – in effect – using it to do some selling for you. But how do you know the impact it has had if you aren't there? How do you know she won't misunderstand it? Or that she'll give it the focus it deserves? How can you respond to any questions that it provokes? How can you have a peer-level discussion about it?

And, let's say you write something that *does* impress her. Well, wouldn't it have been even more impactful if you'd *discussed* it? You could increase her excitement more in a conversation than you ever could with her reading it cold.

Proposals should be a confirmation, not an exploration. In other words, they should *confirm* in writing what you've already agreed verbally. They shouldn't *explore* new things you've never discussed before.

But even if convinced of my logic here, you might still have one lingering concern: 'that's all very well. But just because *I'm* convinced doesn't mean *my customers* will be. Often, they ask me for a proposal before I want to send it to them'.

Yes, this will happen. And, as is often the case, the solution is to have a pre-prepared script that you roll out every time it does. Here's one that works well – notice how I show it's in *her* interest for me not to send the proposal early.

Example script	My script
'Thanks for asking. But I don't yet have a clear idea of how I can best help. I wouldn't want to send you something that isn't the best solution for you. Let's explore things further; and then I'll be able to put it in writing for you'.	

If she agrees, happy days – keep chatting. If she won't entertain this, that's a big red warning flag. She might be saying 'write a proposal' to get you out of the room. So you could be about to waste a lot of time writing something that won't be read. In this case, simply say something like:

Example script	My script
'That won't work for either of us, I'm afraid. I'm happy to discuss things further with you now. Or, if time's tight, we could re-convene. But writing something down before we're agreed will waste both your and my time. What would you suggest we do?'	

If it's still a 'no', save yourself a lot of pain and get out. Remember the Kate Moss Syndrome – just because you find something attractive, doesn't mean you've got a chance with it. Even if this opportunity seems wonderful, being asked to write a proposal by guesswork will almost always lead to a frustrating, pointless waste of time. And Alpha Dogs just don't let that happen to themselves.

Agree your follow-up *before* you send the proposal

How many of your proposals end up in the Black Hole of Doom? That dark, dreadful graveyard where proposals go and never reappear?

You know the type of thing: you send them. The customer doesn't reply. So you chase her. Still no reply. You chase again. Still no reply. You get to the point where you know you could stalk her and follow her home, and you *still* wouldn't get a reply.

So avoid the mistake of attaching a proposal to an email, pressing 'send' and thinking 'job done'.

It isn't.

Proposals are supposed to start something (the project), not end it. So ensure things don't stop with your proposal, or you'll end up with loads in your pipeline. And, with proposals, delays are never good.

Instead, it should work like this:

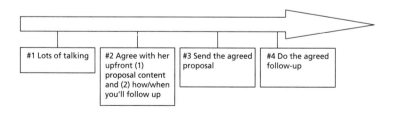

So, after all your conversations (#1 above), agree two things with her (#2):

- The proposal's content (see the next section).
- How/when you'll follow-up later (this section).

So, then, when she gets your agreed proposal (#3), you both already know when you'll be discussing it later (#4).

Once again, know your script to ask for the follow-up in advance. This one's good – after all, everyone hates Telephone Tennis:

Example script	My script
'As agreed, I'll send you the proposal on Wednesday. When would you like us to discuss it, to agree next steps? [early next week] Great. Let's avoid Telephone Tennis, and put a time for us to speak in the diary. When's best for you early next week?' [She gives her preferred time. You send a calendar entry to you both called 'Telephone Meeting: to discuss our proposal about X']	

Agree your proposal content before you send it

If you were writing a proposal for me, what content would I want to see in it?

You don't know, do you?

How could you? You haven't asked me.

Similarly, exactly what information does she want you to put in her proposal? Well, unless you ask her, you won't know – even if you think you do. And, when you don't know, three things happen:

- You guess.
- You write too much.
- You get it wrong anyway.

All pretty painful – for you and her.

So, ask what information she wants you to include. Again, know your script. This one's a belter:

Example script	My script
'The last thing I want to do is bore you with irrelevant information. So, let's agree what the main headings of the proposal should be'.	

I take it you can see why this is so effective? I mean, can you honestly imagine her saying 'No, it's ok. Just be *irrelevant*'?

Also, my script asks her to agree the proposal's *headings*. Once I know them, it's easier and more pleasant to write. I don't have to spend ages guessing and/or throwing the kitchen sink at her. Best of all, when she opens it, it's *exactly* what she was expecting. This ties in to what we agreed earlier: proposals should be a confirmation, not an exploration.

Of course, there are certain things that *you* will want to include in your proposal – despite what she says. So, after she's told you what she wants, use prompting questions to raise these with her:

Example script	My script
'I'll structure the proposal so it contains everything we've just agreed.	
To make sure we cover everything that's important, let me just check something: a few of my customers have also asked me to include X, Y and Z in their proposals. Would you find these helpful too?'	

You'll see what X, Y and Z might be in the next section. They *aren't* your sales credentials though. Here's why …

A proven proposal template to use as is and/or copy bits from

Yes, you want the proposal to contain the information she wants.

But sometimes she'll ask your opinion on what it should contain.

Or she'll say 'I don't mind – write whatever you want'.

Or she might ask you to include only a couple of things – say, deliverables and price – which you don't think is a good enough reflection of the value you're looking to achieve together.

So, it's useful to have a standard format in mind. That way, you can use it either:

- As your proposal template if she asks you to choose what goes into it.
- To prompt you, to check with her you've both covered everything.

When thinking what this content might be, it's best to think what customers tend to want to know, and work backwards from there. This is much better than pages and pages discussing how brilliant your sales credentials are – something she's already convinced of or you wouldn't have got this far in your discussions.

This table shows what you want the customer to think, then works backwards to suggest what a good proposal should contain, and possible titles for each section.

What you want the customer to think …	Therefore, your proposal must contain …	Titles you'll use in the proposal itself
'I want to open this document.'	A compelling title.	It depends on the project – but probably something including her #1 AFTER.
'I need to do something – and I need to do it with these guys, nobody else.'	A short section, outlining the customer's pain-point.	The need for change.
'Yes, these are the objectives and measures that I agreed.'	The objectives and measures you discussed – using the customer's words as much as possible.	Our objectives and measures.
'Yes, that's the value I want the project to deliver.'	The value you will deliver to the customer (ideally, a £value, so she has something concrete to compare your £price to).	The value our work will bring.
'Yes, that's the project I agreed to'.	The timeline plan you co-created.	Our implementation plan: how we will deliver your objectives.

What you want the customer to think …	Therefore, your proposal must contain …	Titles you'll use in the proposal itself
'I know exactly when this is going to start, and what it will look like when it does.'	Lots of detail on the first thing the customer will see when the project starts. This helps encourage her to give a speedy acceptance!	How – and when – we will start our project.
'I know what they'll be doing; and what I need to do.'	An outline of who is responsible for what. Great for showing that you have expectations of her as well, since you're both Alpha Dogs.	Confirmation of who is responsible for what.
'Yes – let's start.'	A choice of yeses. In other words, don't say 'It's £100k. Want it or not?' – she might say 'not.' Instead, offer 2 or 3 options, for her to select one from.	Options, prices, terms and conditions.
'I know what to do to accept this proposal; and it's very easy.'	Clear guidance on what she should do to accept the project.	Acceptance/ confirmation of next steps.

This table's right hand column shows what your proposal headings might be. To help you see how these might look in practice, I've written two versions below:

1. A completed proposal, to show you how it might look in real life.
2. A standard template you can use some/all of, to create future proposals.

Remember: the customer – or you – might not want it in this format. This is just to give you an idea of how a proposal might work (this structure also often works well for an Executive Summary at the start of a much larger proposal).

Proposal: Helping X Ltd increase sales through better negotiating

1. The need for change

Your competition is taking market share from you. This has knocked your sales team's confidence. As a direct consequence, they have started offering big discounts early in their negotiations, to make sure they win the sale. This has already cost you over £1 million in profits – a number that will escalate.

As agreed, it is therefore essential to both:
- Improve your messaging to the marketplace, to remind them of the value that your firm brings.
- Improve your sales team's skills and confidence to charge appropriate prices, and not discount too early.

This proposal confirms how we've agreed to work together to deliver these results.

---

2. Our objectives and measures

Our objectives of the project, and how we will know we have achieved them, include:

Objectives (what we want to achieve)	Measures (how we'll know we've achieved them)
Improve your messaging, to better convey the value-add to the marketplace.	• More inbound opportunities. • Improved customer engagement scores in your customer survey.
To stop the sales team offering big discounts early.	• Less discounts! • Improved profit margins. • Less pace in the pipeline. We want a return to the previous levels, before they started discounting early to bring quick sales.
To equip the sales team with more skills and confidence to sell well in the current marketplace.	• More meetings with prospects. • Better conversion rates. • More repeat sales to existing customers. • More referrals to new customers.

3. The value our work will bring

We agreed a successful outcome for this project is worth in the region of £5–10 million. We calculated this by reviewing your losses to date, and doing a simple extrapolation exercise (please let me know if you want me to forward our workings on this).

(continued)

But this project is not just about the numbers. Other valuable benefits include:

- Their improved confidence will help break the current inertia on the sales floor. More of them will be out meeting customers and making more calls.
- Our work to embed best practices will ensure their learnings stay with the team long after our project's end date.
- Improved press coverage, as we get your new messaging out to your target market.

4. Our implementation plan: how we will deliver your objectives

Our discussions showed the following to be the best way to achieve your objectives:

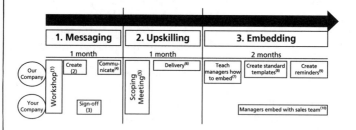

Notes

    (1) Workshop – see section 5 below.

    (2) We create your messaging using our findings from the workshop.

    (3) You sign-off this messaging – or we adjust it to reflect your feedback, then you sign-off.

    (4) We formalize the messaging, including embedding it in all your sales and marketing material. We communicate these to all relevant stakeholders – your leaders first; then your sales team; then your customers.

(5) We meet again to scope the upskilling phase – to agree content, delivery mechanisms, timings etc.

(6) We train your sales team, covering the topics we agreed during the scoping meeting.

(7) Your managers will make or break this project. So we upskill them how to role model and embed the new behaviours, including how to coach team members who revert.

(8) & (9) We create templates and reminders to support your managers and their teams.

(10) Your managers coach their teams – with our support – until 'the new way' has become 'the way'.

5. How – and when – we'll start your project

The first step of our project is the messaging workshop – note 1 above. During it, we will:

- Discuss customer feedback from your recent survey.
- Discuss feedback from our survey of your salespeople.
- Agree the approach we'll take to creating your new messaging.
- Discuss early concepts, to help us create the messaging quickly for you.

To confirm timings: we can start this project as soon as you confirm you wish to proceed. It will last approximately four months after this date.

6. Confirmation of who is responsible for what

This project requires both our companies to take responsibility and ownership for our respective areas, as detailed in section 4's timeline.

Your key contacts from our firm are:
- Alan Adams, relationship partner, responsible for overseeing the project, and ensuring we achieve your objectives in the timescales agreed.

(continued)

- Brenda Bellows, messaging consultant, responsible for the creation of your new messaging.
- Charlie Cook, training consultant, responsible for the delivery of the training and embedding phases.

As per our discussions, you will ensure all relevant stakeholders turn up to meetings with us on time, and prepared.

7. Options, prices, terms and conditions

We discussed two approaches we could take to this project:
- Option 1 – we do everything in section 4's timeline – £315,000.
- Option 2 – we do both the messaging and the training phases, but you take ownership for the embedding phase – £195,000.

Our terms and conditions are on the attached schedule.

8. Agreement/confirmation of next steps

We have a call scheduled for 10 am on Wednesday, where we will confirm next steps.

Should you want to formally accept this proposal before then, please email your confirmation, including which option you've chosen.

I look forward to speaking to you on Wednesday.

Alan Adams
Email: Alan@YLtd.com
Mobile: 07712 345678

Taking out all the specifics in the above example, the blank template you can use for your future opportunities is:

Proposal: helping [customer name] [achieve #1 AFTER]

1. The need for change

The *[situation/recent change]* has led to *[bad thing/good opportunity]*. The impact of this is *[ramification for the customer if they do nothing]*.

As agreed, it is therefore essential to *[improvement your project will deliver]*. This will directly cause *[positive impact you will bring]*.

This proposal confirms how we've agreed to work together to deliver these results.

2. Our objectives and measures

Our objectives of the project, and how we will know we have achieved them, include:

Objectives (what we want to achieve)	Measures (how we'll know we've achieved them)
[insert]	[insert]
[insert]	[insert]
[insert]	[insert]

3. The value our work will bring

We agreed a successful outcome from our work together is worth *[£range]*. We calculated this by *[explain where the range came from]*.

(continued)

But this project is not just about the numbers. Other valuable benefits include:

- [insert other benefit]
- [insert other benefit]
- [insert other benefit]

4. Our implementation plan: how we'll deliver your objectives

Our discussions showed the following to be the best way to achieve your objectives:

[Insert timeline visual, with supporting notes]

5. How – and when – we'll start your project

The first step of our project is *[first step on above timeline]*. During this [*step*], we will:

- [Detail]
- [Detail]
- [Detail]

To confirm timings: we can start our project as soon as you confirm you wish to proceed. It will last approximately [*duration*] after this date.

6. Confirmation of who is responsible for what

This project requires both our companies to take responsibility and ownership for our respective areas, as detailed in section 4's timeline.

Your key contacts from [*your firm*] are:

- [Name, position, responsible for x]
- [Name, position, responsible for y]

In addition, [*their company name*] is also responsible for [*their responsibility*].

7. Options, prices, terms and conditions

We discussed [*number*] approaches we could take to this project:

- Option 1 – we do all the deliverables in section 4's timeline – [£*x*].
- Option 2 – we do everything in the timeline, except [*deliverable 1*] and [*deliverable 2*] – [£*y*].
- Option 3 – ?

Our terms and conditions are [*list them here if they're simple; direct her to a document if they're more complex*].

8. Agreement/confirmation of next steps

We have a call scheduled for [*time*] on [*date*] to confirm next steps.

Should you want to formally accept this proposal before then, please email your confirmation, including which option you've chosen.

I look forward to speaking to you on [*date*].

[*Your name*]

[*Your contact details*]

Ensure all your accompanying communications are brilliant

So that's how to write a brilliant proposal.

However, even if you do write something brilliant, it's still not enough. There's one final piece of the jigsaw – often overlooked, but very important. To show what I mean, here's a true story to strike fear into the heart of anyone who thinks it's ok to cut corners with proposals …

I once helped a consultant write a proposal for a big project. It was worth a lot of money to him. It would have been his biggest ever contract.

The proposal was really good. It covered everything his customer said she'd wanted. It was well written.

But he didn't win the work.

When he asked why not, she said she was so underwhelmed by his covering email that she didn't feel she could trust him with such an important project. Her exact words: *'if you don't take care of little things like emails when you know I'm watching, how can I trust you to take care of big things when you don't think I am?'*

Ouch.

I asked him to send me this covering email. It said …

Title: FYI
See attached
Cheers,
NAME

Dreadful.

And what a *waste*.

We'd created this wonderful proposal. If the customer had just read it, he'd have had an outstanding chance of winning the business. But all our effort was ruined by the first thing she saw: his covering email. I wouldn't even have noticed his email in my inbox. Would you?

Invest time ensuring your emails impress. Here's one approach that works well:

Title: Jane, our proposal to help X Ltd increase sales through better negotiating

Jane,

As requested, I attach our proposal showing how we can equip your sales team with the skills and confidence to increase sales through better negotiating.

You'll see it contains all the main points we discussed. In particular:

- The value our project will deliver for you and for X Ltd.
- A detailed timeline, showing what you can expect to happen, by when.
- Two options, for you to choose how you wish to proceed.

As agreed, I'll ring you at 10 am on Wednesday to agree our next steps. If you want to discuss before then, please call my mobile – 07712 345678.

Best,

Alan

You'll notice:

- The title is compelling. She'll open the email.
- It starts with 'As requested' (or similar). This reminds her that she's already agreed to getting it in this format, and that you've written the document she wanted.

- Briefly mentioning two or three highlights means she's more likely to open the proposal, to read the detail.
- There's a clear call to action, reminding her there's a pre-agreed next step.
- By providing your contact details, you're empowering her to increase the pace if she wants to.
- The email's short, but contains enough to persuade her to open the attachment. You don't need to re-write half your proposal. But neither can you write only 'see attached'.
- Let's face it: it doesn't take long to write an email like this. It only takes minutes – seconds? – to do. But, if you don't, you might find you've wasted all the hours and days you've spent getting this far.

Let's assume she opens your email. And that she loves your proposal. If so, you might well get the dream response 'Yes. That's brilliant. Start'.

However, of course, you'll sometimes have one final hurdle: the sales presentation. The next chapter shows how to deliver a winning one.

Doggie Treats

Write a compelling proposal/business case

- If everything else has gone well so far, proposals should be relatively straightforward.
- Proposals should be a confirmation, not an exploration.
- Agree beforehand:
  - What the proposal's section headings will be.
  - When you'll discuss it later (thus avoiding the Black Hole of Doom).
- Use this chapter's template – or one that works for you – to help you write future proposals.
- Ensure your covering email is as impressive as your proposals.

8
Become Top Dog (2)

Nail the final presentation

The opening words to a presentation that make my toes curl are heard way too often:

'I know this slide is a bit busy, and you won't be able to read it, but …'

But what?

Why are you showing me a slide I can't read?

Isn't the whole point of a slide to simplify or support compelling messages? A picture paints a thousand words. But a thousand words do *not* paint a good picture. Especially if you can't read them.

And, even when slides are OK, delivery often isn't. For example, reading from notes – or worse, rehearsing your notes so you're word-perfect – often makes you look like a mouthpiece. This makes your presentation a 'verbal document' rather than a discussion led by a knowledgeable expert. It also demonstrates a lack of confidence. It's Beta Dog behaviour.

And people *hate* sitting through this sort of presentation. You do. I do. *Everyone* does. In fact, a very senior Audit

Committee Chairman once told me 'I never read slide packs sent in advance. They're a waste of time. I've never learnt anything from one. I want to engage with the supplier, ask good questions and get insightful responses. That is the test of someone who truly understands their topic'.

Here's a much better way to start

I once startled a team of consultants who'd asked me to open an important presentation to a major bank. I was given the slides in the taxi on the way there. It was competent; it was clear; it was compelling. It was dull.

They'd sent it to the customer two days earlier. So I opened by saying 'You've seen our slide deck. You've read our proposal. Proposals and slide packs are necessary, but dull. Rather than take you on a death march through materials you've already seen, I'd rather we use this session to focus discussion on what the critical factors are, and how we can best work together to make sure we deliver outstanding results'.

The presentation became a peer-to-peer exchange of views on the reality of making the project work. It was completely free-form, with the customer hugely engaged, and our team able to demonstrate real depth and expertise.

Afterwards they fed back 'We formed a team with you in that room. It was so refreshing to talk *as a team* about what really mattered. It was 180 degrees different from the formulaic presentations from your competitors. You'd won before you left the room'.

Using our language, this was confident Alpha Dog behaviour that differentiated us, and won us a huge strategic engagement. And it was the introduction that set us up for success. Infinitely better than 'founded in 1922', closely followed by a map of your offices.

Dramatically improve your presentations

There are many topics I could cover about presentations – from the major (how to be interesting) to the more trivial (what to do with your hands). But I want to keep my advice – and the length of the book – manageable. So I'm focusing on:

- Major things people get wrong …
- … that are easy to fix.

There are six:

1. Be interesting.
2. Be two-way – think 'chat, not rant'.
3. Good questions, and even better answers.
4. Visuals that enhance your message, not dilute/ contradict it.
5. Structure it right.
6. Start and finish brilliantly.

Looking at each in turn …

1. How to be interesting

Since most people's presentations are dull, it's pretty easy to ensure yours stand out as being interesting.

To achieve this, start by thinking what people find interesting. For instance, they like:

- Interactivity – everyone would rather join in a dialogue, than listen to someone talk *at* them.
- Interesting stories.
- Brevity.
- To learn something new.
- Good visuals.
- Interesting quotations.
- Variety.

You could expand this list by adding the opposite of what people hate. For instance, since people hate wordy slides, using sparse slides would make you more interesting. So, your list might also include:

- Sparse slides (not wordy).
- Good headings (not boring ones like 'about us' and 'our experience').
- Minimal background information, especially at the start (thus avoiding the tedious 10-slide scene-set).
- Relevance (in presentations, is there anything worse than your audience looking at you and thinking 'I don't need to know this'?)

Now that you know what *others* find interesting, identify what *you* could do, to be more like the list. For instance, if you want your presentations to be more interactive, you could ask more questions. Your list might now look like this:

People like ... (The theory)	Actions you could take, to be more like this ... (The practice)
Interactivity	• Ask questions.
Stories	• Prepare relevant WWFs in advance. • Practise, test and refine them until they're very good.
Brevity	• Remove as much content as possible.
To learn something new	• Teach them something new. • Ask experts for their input.
Good visuals	• Use them – pictures, flowcharts, tables, graphs – *anything* that isn't just words. • When it matters, use professional designers to ensure they impress.
Interesting quotations	• Use quotations that you/your colleagues like. • Use Google to find quotation websites, input your keywords and see which quotations come up. For any you like, learn more about the author, source and context, so you can tell the story.
Variety	• Check your presentation isn't all the same. If you have, say, five consecutive identical-looking slides, insert something from this table into the middle, to break it up. • Ask yourself 'when will they be bored?' Then change it, so they aren't.

(continued)

People like ... (The theory)	Actions you could take, to be more like this ... (The practice)
Sparse slides	• Remove as many words as possible from wordy slides. Or start with a blank slide and write only your key words on there. • Use interesting layouts – a box round each phrase, a flowchart etc.
Good headings	• Use interesting headings, not the usual 'background', 'about us', 'our technology.' • A simple improvement: use 'how' and their AFTER. So 'our technology' becomes 'How our technology will transform your competitive advantage.'
Minimal background information	• Ask them beforehand what information they want to see ... • ... or assume it's none. You wouldn't have got this far if they didn't know your background.
Relevant	• Ask beforehand 'what would you like us to cover in our presentation to you?' • Where appropriate, share your proposed structure upfront, and ask for any changes they'd like to see.

This table isn't exhaustive. But it's a good start. In fact, it's such a good start you might think 'how on earth am I going to do all that?'

Well, you don't have to do 'all that'. But, to be more interesting than the competition, you'll have to do more than none of it.

2. How to be two-way – think 'chat, not rant'

Questions make or break a presentation. If you don't ask any, they won't speak. If they don't ask any, they aren't interested.

So you *must* get them talking.

I know this sounds obvious. But when people prepare presentations, they usually:

1. Script the content.
2. Prepare the slides.
3. Practise saying the content.

And that's it.

But where are the questions? There's no interactivity. Instead, the steps should be

1. Script the content.
2. Script the questions.
3. Prepare the slides.
4. Practise saying the content *and asking the questions.*

Questions are particularly important early, since they set the tone for the meeting being a two-way dialogue. Use simple ones to kick things off. For example:

Example script	My script
'Our discussions so far have shown that you want to achieve X, Y and Z. Are they still the key outcomes for you? Or has anything else come up since our last conversation?'	

As for questions to use *during* the presentation: there are lots of examples throughout the book. Choose your favourites. Practise asking them before the day. Don't hope they'll come out right when it matters – they won't. Remember: if you don't know what you're going to ask, you won't ask anything. You'll just keep talking.

And one final technique to ensure you're asking enough questions:

- Review your presentation notes.
- Use a highlighter pen to show when you intend to ask questions.
- See how much highlighting you've done. You need:
  - lots at the start – to start them talking; and
  - no major gaps in the middle – or they'll stop.
- Plug any long gaps with 'get them talking' questions – 'before we carry on, have you any questions?' or 'before we carry on, what are your thoughts so far? We're particularly interested in what you like about what we've said, and also any initial concerns you might have'.

3. Good questions, and even better answers

A rule of thumb: they will always ask the question you're dreading.

So don't let them.

Here's how …

Your ability to answer tricky questions is a big differentiator. This means a key part of your preparation must be to identify the questions you're most likely to get – including the ones you're dreading – and then script, fine-tune and rehearse persuasive responses.

So far, so obvious. But now for a magic tip – something that virtually nobody does – one that can take you from losing to winning in *minutes*.

As you review likely questions, you'll see some centre on their concerns/objections. The magic tip: pre-empt and remove these concerns during your presentation. In other words, *you raise them yourself* – 'I know that some of you have concerns about the costs of doing this. Let me put your minds at rest by showing that …'

If you don't pre-empt it, they might ask questions about it. And you can guarantee they'll ask at the wrong time or in the wrong way. This puts you on the defensive, looking to recover lost ground. One question from them can turn you into a Beta Dog desperate to reassure.

Even worse, they might *not* ask it. This means they'll leave the room still concerned. This will be followed – a few days later – with a phone call 'I'm sorry, you came a close second. We were just too worried about the cost'.

To pre-empt successfully, simply:

- Identify the concern – in this example, cost.
- Write your response – your answer about providing Return On Investment, or some such.
- Script how you'll bring it up – 'I know that many of you …' or 'some of our most successful customers

were originally worried about X. Is that the case with you?'
- Script how you'll end it – 'how does that feel to you?'

You won't do this with every single concern/question you identified. But you must do it with the two or three main ones which, if unresolved, will ruin your chances of winning.

4. Create visuals that enhance your message, not dilute/contradict it

Good companies don't use rubbish visuals. Of course they don't. They're *good* companies. Using anything rubbish doesn't make sense. It isn't congruent. And it triggers worrying thoughts in the buyer's mind: 'If they can't be bothered to use spellcheck, how can I trust them with the finer details of my £multi-million project?'

I've already given you lots of guidance about visuals in this book so far. Here's a reminder of some of the main ones:

- Only use visuals if they aid discussion. When they don't – which is often – don't use them.
- They're supposed to help explain things to your audience, not remind you what to say. If you want notes, use hand-held cards, not the big shiny screen-shaped thing the audience is looking at.
- Use minimal wording – slides are *not* supposed to be a chopped-up document.
- They must look impressive – get them designed.

- It's always useful when they've seen the visual before – 'ah, I recognize that'. For example, the co-created timeline works well in final presentations.
- Hand-drawn visuals can still be powerful, even at this late stage of discussions.

And be creative with them. If you aren't the creative type, ask someone who is. For example, imagine a buyer was choosing between two plumbers. Her brief said 'please show how your process works'.

One showed this …

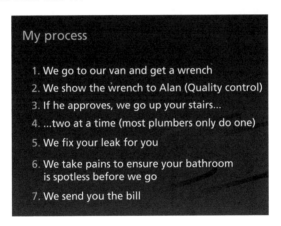

The other, this …

Who'd win the work?

The second one, yes?

It's actually the same plumber. That's the difference a visual can make.

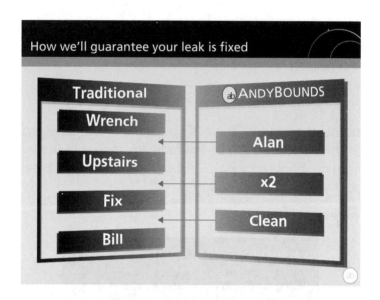

5. Structure it right

Good news: there's nothing new for you to learn about this. The presentation structure simply follows the same order as your proposal in the previous chapter:

- Compelling title on Slide 1 – include their #1 AFTER.
- The need for change.
- Our objectives and measures.
- The value our work will bring.
- Our implementation plan: how we will deliver your objectives.
- How – and when – we will start our project.
- Confirmation of who is responsible for what.
- Options.
- Next steps.

You will, of course, add new bits in relevant places – a discussion about any new OMG critical factors, new obstacles and how to remove them, and so on. You might also choose not to use some sections. But the overall structure is pretty much the same.

6. Start and finish brilliantly

It's absolutely essential to start well. They must engage instantly. If they don't then they might never do.

In fact, the start is so important I suggest people spend 20% of their prep time on the first 2% of their presentation. Win them over then, and you'll probably win overall. Lose them then, and it's game over.

I gave an example of a great opening before. Here it is again. How would you tweak it, so it sounds more like you?

Example script	My script
'You've seen our slide deck. You've read our proposal. Proposals and slide packs are necessary, but dull.	
Rather than take you on a death march through materials you've already seen, I'd rather we use this session to focus discussion on what the critical factors are, and how we can best work together to make sure we deliver outstanding results'.	

And finally: make sure you end powerfully. Not the feeble 'any questions?', or 'thank you so much for seeing us'. Instead, state with certainty that you want the work, and remind them of the AFTERs they'll get.

Example script	My script
'We are certain we can deliver the outcomes you want. We've done so many times before, like with [example X] and [example Y]. We are also convinced the project plan we've created together will help you achieve [AFTERs X, Y and Z]. We can start as soon as you confirm you'd like us to. Do you have any final questions for us before we leave?'	

And that's it.

We've come on a long journey together. The book started with how to get the meeting. This chapter's ended with how to get the sale.

There's only one area left for us to master: yes, you now know what to do. The final chapter shows how to make sure you always do it.

Doggie Treats

Nail the final sales presentation

- Presentations are a great opportunity for differentiation – because most people's are so poor.
- Although it's called a 'presentation', it isn't just you *presenting* stuff. Instead, it should be a two-way conversation.
- It's important both you and they ask each other good questions. So take steps in your planning to ensure this happens.
- Use visuals that enhance your message. If you aren't sure whether to include a particular visual, leave it out. This forces you to chat about the topic. If you include it, you both end up reading something that probably wasn't needed.
- Use your proposal structure to guide your presentation structure.
- Ensure you start and finish brilliantly by scripting and rehearsing your opening and closing lines.

Stay Top Dog

Lose your fear, and win more

When we started this book, we had one clear focus: to cause AFTERs.

So yes, we wanted you to enjoy reading it and to learn new approaches. But our key focus always was:

'How can we make it easy for you to do things better AFTER reading it?'

That's why we've given you so many scripts, step-by-step guides, lists of questions, word-for-word answers to common objections, templates to follow, and the like – so you can use them *immediately*.

We're now coming to the end of our book. So our question is:

What bits will you use first, AFTER reading it?

Your answer will depend on various things of course – your business, your priorities, your interests, your strengths. But, most importantly, your *habits*. The easiest way to explain this – and what you can do about it – is with one final, quick dog analogy …

Brook spends too much time in the cellar. It's very comfortable there – three dog cages, a basket, all full of comfortable cushions and old duvets. She ventures out if there might be food of any kind on offer; and often does this timidly. But at the slightest noise, she scampers quickly back to her comfort zone – the cellar. But tell her it's 'walkies', and she's as excited as a dog can be. She rushes into the garden and has the time of her life.

Misty's the opposite. She loves being with the family – or anyone really. She sits in a dog bed watching TV with us, and loves to bark at other dogs on the screen. Understandably, she gets twice as much attention as Brook – yes, partly because she's so sociable. But mainly because she's actually there. She's front-of-mind because she's front-of-face.

Are you more like Brook or Misty? Do you stay in the office 'comfort zone cellar' more often than go out talking to people?

We tell ourselves these comfort zones are comfortable. But they aren't really. They're more like Habit Zones – we do these things because we always do them, rather than because they're what's best for us (this is the same as when people say they use PowerPoint as a *comfort* blanket, and – in the same sentence – say they don't feel *comfortable* using it! That's habit, not comfort).

If *you* stay in the office more than go out, is it comfortable or habitual?

I ask because there are no customers in the office – except on the end of a phone. And there's little excitement to be had in the office unless you're preparing for a great customer meeting, or inspiring your team and others around you.

When you do activities like these, it makes your working day a brilliant day. And if that *is* what your working day is usually like – loads of great meetings and conversations – I'm not surprised you stay in so much.

Except I bet it isn't.

Instead, we arrive at our desks. We process emails. We attend internally focused meetings that always last an hour and always have too many people there. We bitch about our bosses. We read interminable internal newsletters. We moan about the latest restructuring. Our very life force is sucked from us. We begin to lose the will to live. We certainly lose the will for others to live. We long for the weekend … even though it's only Tuesday morning.

And why do we focus on these sapping, mood-hoovering activities? Habit? Because it's easy and we can?

How much better our working lives would be if we dropped these habits – these negative, time-absorbing habits – and focused on:

- Arranging and preparing for great customer interactions.
- Helping and inspiring others to do so.

The most successful people do this: so we should

I once listened to a motivational speaker who won an Olympic gold medal for rowing.

What resonated most was his story about how they stopped doing anything that wouldn't 'make the boat go faster'. As simple as that. If something would make the boat go faster, they did it. If not, they wouldn't. That even included missing the opening ceremony!

The best advice we could ever give you: shift your energy and focus away from the negative (emails and admin) to the life-enhancing (exciting customer and colleague interactions).

Help yourself get into the *habit* of doing so, by regularly asking of new activities 'yes, but will this make my boat go faster?'. If yes, do it. If not, don't – and refocus onto something that will.

For example, these activities will all make your boat go faster:

- Call a target contact and arrange a meeting.
- Write some great WWF stories for the meetings you already have in the diary.
- Go and get some new WWF material from colleagues.
- Meet and inspire colleagues.
- Ask the Office Superstar for top tips about how they go about their day.
- Write a list and execute more customer-related actions.

- Use recurring diary reminders to help you break your habits and embed new ones – these could be skills-based reminders ('still using AFTERs?') or emotional ('still having fun?').

Best of all: get out of the office. Go and see someone. If you need to build your confidence for this, start with people who you know and like, and then go from there.

You don't have to do all these ideas I'm suggesting. But, if you want to enjoy your job more, you'll have to do more than none.

And finally, let's look at this from a different angle. Imagine that you *did* master doing this. That you got into good habits that helped you enjoy your job more. That you lived your life surrounded by talking, walking real people, rather than being in the seemingly-comfortable-yet-stifling cellar.

Do this, and your colleagues and customers would start to see a more energized, upbeat, positive, successful and – most importantly – happier-at-work you.

You might then be able to help *them* become invigorated, as they seek your guidance and coaching. This would help them become more successful.

Keep doing this and you change the mindset and culture of your team, your department – even your organization.

Most life-changing of all: you could inspire your families, partners and friends too.

And that is the absolute best thing a Top Dog could ever do.

Doggie Treats

Lose your fear and win more

- The most important thing about this book is what you do AFTER reading it.
- Staying in the office all day might feel like a *Comfort* Zone. But it isn't always that *comfortable*. It's more of a Habit Zone.
- So break your habits. Get out of the office more. Go and see people you want to spend time with. You'll both be delighted you did.

get more

Articles + interviews
Videos + podcasts
Books + blogs
Authors +inspiration

08225 09/09